The Dirty Business of Being a Zookeeper

Rhonda Barbut

Copyright © 2025

The moral right to be identified as the creators of the work has been asserted by them in accordance with the Copyright, Designs and Patents Act 1988. All rights reserved.

No part of this book may be reproduced, stored in a retrieval system or transmitted in any form or by any means, electronic, mechanical, photocopying, recording or otherwise, without the prior permission of the author.

Book Cover by 100 Covers

Images: Owl photo on front and back cover photo by Graham Hay and snake photo on front cover by Henderson Photographics

Designed by Red Feather Publishing

www.redfeather.com.au

ISBN for print: 978-1-7641325-0-3

ISBN for ebook: 978-1-7641325-1-0

I dedicate this book to my mother. In 1998, she came out to see me in Australia and adored the kangaroos.

Contents

About the Author	3
Bugger! Off to Court We Must Go	5
1. Zoos	7
2. My Childhood	18
3. The Magpies Started This Journey	21
4. The Zookeeper's Role	30
5. Now a Zookeeper	53
6. Mike Now a Zookeeper	60
7. It's an Amazing Job	69
8. It's a Smelly Job	129
9. It's a Dangerous Job	133
10. It's a Competitive Job	154
11. The Underbelly of the Zoo World	158
12. Rhonda and Mike	186
13. For Us All to Believe in Zoos	198

14.	Now Let's Go to Court	224
15.	Life after Being a Zookeeper	228
16.	A New Generation of Zookeepers	238
17.	So You Want to Be a Zookeeper?	240
18.	Our Do's and Don'ts for Aspiring Zookeepers	243
19.	Zookeepers Make the News	249
20.	Acknowledgement	253

'The only creature on earth whose natural habitat in a zoo is the Zookeeper.' – Robert Brault, Author

Dedication

To everyone around the world who are animal lovers and work with animals, either paid or as volunteers, thank you for the passion, drive, dedication and life commitment you have to make animals have a better place on this planet. Your voice to improve the conditions for animals, to rescue, treat, care, raise, or rehome whatever the species, is so important. Our tribe in the animal world has highs and lows, heaps of disappointments at times, but being dedicated, and by working together, we can make a difference 'by going the extra mile', improving existing conditions wherever we live in the world.

About the Author

As two trained, skilled, qualified and experienced Zookeepers, I and my partner Mike hold over 40 years' knowledge of working in the animal field, including 10 zoos in Australia and internationally. As such, we can offer a deep and honest insight of what really happens behind the scenes as a Zookeeper. I wrote this book as a real survival guide to working as a Zookeeper. It may be a reality check for anyone who wants to know what a Zookeeper position entails in this challenging jungle. I have pulled together all our experiences of working in the Zoo World, working with good mentors, other experienced Zookeepers, Senior Zookeepers, Head Keepers and Curators, past and present. *Whilst writing this book, I have our tame Eclectus parrot sitting on my shoulder supervising my dialogue.*

I have shared our highs with the lows, and pointed out how important zoos can be for everyone to visit. I have thrown in some 'food for thought' as well as our opinion of why we say YES to having good zoos that keep high standards. Being a Zookeeper can be a tough job, and it may come as a surprise to the public that it's not all cute and fluffy in this habitat.

Both of us started in the industry in 1998 and did not know each other until 10 years later when I returned from working overseas, to gain work back at the original zoo here in WA. Through this book, I want to give the readers some insight into this specialised environment, the real dirt—the bullshit—with some humour too, on this exciting, unique job, but it's an exhausting journey of working not just as a Zookeeper, but as a *great* Zookeeper.

Bugger! Off to Court We Must Go

A year after we left the zoo world, we woke up at 5 am to drive 200 km to get to the 'big smoke' of the city. We parked in a soulless underground car park in this concrete jungle. Next to our dusty, dirty 4 x 4, that looked so out of place, we stripped into our smart official clothing, definitely not our usual rig. We felt out of our comfort zone but having each other was assuring. We now looked the part and joined all the 'city slickers' in the hectic rush hour. It felt like one big ant march. We were greeted by two familiar faces amongst the busy Industrial Magistrates Court of Western Australia. Our lawyer and barrister took the lead thankfully as it wasn't the natural environment for two Zookeepers.

We were in court regarding some management not supporting qualified experienced Zookeepers in their positions, in fact making it impossible and not taking our position seriously. Unless you work within this field, you may not be aware, or understand the importance of us doing this, but if you love animals, you will. We were confident that our legal representatives were fighting hard for us in this battle. The Magistrate entered the court; we stood up, and the proceeds began. All the legal jargon went over our heads—the whole system can be frustrating—but we sat with respect, hoping that as Zookeepers, we could express that 'animal lives matter'. We managed to get through this pretrial in one piece, even though the sterile place made us feel anxious. That's one down of many pretrial court hearings, before the trial starts. This experience confirmed why most ex-Zookeepers never take action against organisations and just walk away.

As we drove home in our normal attire of Hard Yakka uniform (khaki pants and shirts), we pondered on how we got to this place—two great, experienced, devoted and passionate Zookeepers fighting a legal battle against non-animal people that caused us so much stress whilst working in a local authority-run zoo. Fortunately, our journey working in zoos was not always like this. It was an exciting journey, never dull, filled with amazing moments and, of course, the animals were the ultimate thrill. This was the only kind of dirt, animal dirt, we wanted to work in, but here we are, wasting valuable time, playing with filthy human dirt and welfare issues.

Zoos

Whilst growing up in the UK, there were plenty of zoos to visit. It was a big day out and some of my best memories are spending time with my grandparents at a good local zoo, which will always be special to me. I fondly remember the mishaps whilst being surrounded by cheeky animals, like when the goat started to eat my best dress and watching a lion play games and then turn and piss like a firehose onto the public, making everyone scamper for their lives! The naughty monkeys picking their noses, or sometimes their bums, with the pure innocence of children, giggling and appreciating all the other species on a fun day out. Now as adults, we can still enjoy a visit to a good zoo, but we do have a lot more questions regarding this traditional attraction.

Zoos are a very old tradition, and an interesting fact I found is that 'Animal Collections' requiring Wild Animal Caretakers or Zookeepers have existed since approximately 3,000 B.C.

Early civilizations in Iraq, Egypt, China and India allowed rulers and their wealthy-class citizens to keep collections of wild animals.

The oldest zoo in the world is in Vienna, Austria and it was established in 1752 and is still running very successfully. I have not had the chance to visit this particular zoo, but I have worked in or visited heaps of zoos over the years, so have gained a good insight into knowing what makes a good zoo and what doesn't.

Let's learn more about zoos before we can make a good judgment.

So, What Is the Meaning of 'Zoo'?

'Zoo' is defined as 'an establishment which maintains a collection of wild animals, typically in a park or gardens for study, conservation or display to the public'. The other terms and titles used for a collection of animals are wildlife parks, conservation centres, sanctuaries, menagerie and aquarium. After doing some research, I have found that there are zoos everywhere in the world, some in rich countries and some in poor countries and yes, zoos are still popular in 2025.

Recently, it came to light that the oldest zoo in Malaysia was closed in 2020 and reopened recently in 2024 and on the first day it drew almost 20,000 visitors. Wow, that is amazing! It's known that zoos and aquariums are some of the most popular tourist attractions with an estimated 700 million visitors globally each year. The proof is in the pudding—I don't think they're going to disappear in the near future. So, with this thought, we can only keep improving the standards for the animals, Zookeepers and visitors, and we certainly know that zoos have changed for the better over the years. I would like to reassure that all the animals displayed at a zoo are cared for by dedicated Zookeepers like myself and my partner. These animals are for the community, for everyone to learn and enjoy, hopefully in a positive manner, with a good unforgettable experience.

It is obvious to me that zoos are still very much part of many people's lives, so with this information, I dug further and found out that there are heaps of zoos—approximately 10,000 zoos/wildlife parks around the world, including 350 in the UK and 200 in Australia. The USA has the most zoos in the world.

One of the biggest and most visited zoos is Disney World in Florida, having over 13 million visitors a year. San Diego Zoo was awarded one of the best zoos in the world, and it was one of the first zoos to have open air cageless exhibits, having over 5 million visitors a year. Singapore Zoo is up there as one of the best zoos with over 2 million visitors a year. London Zoo has over 1 million visitors a year. Perth Zoo has over 700,000 visitors a year. The largest zoo in the world is in Canada, over 700 acres in size. One of the smallest zoos in the UK is just 1 acre and holds a large collection of species. Surprisingly, the zoo that holds the most species of animals in the world is Moscow Zoo. Note: This is the number of species not individual animals.

Most Zookeepers are out there in the background, but the most famous Zookeeper in the world changed all that—Steve Irwin, here in Australia. He became very popular around the world due to his passion for animals. Steve showed the world how important his position as a Zookeeper was, through delivering exciting education on conservation which he achieved every day within the zoo and also through his public events and TV shows. His legacy continues to do this for every Zookeeper on the planet. In the USA, the most famous Zookeepers are Jack Hanna and Ron Magill, and the most famous Zookeeper in the UK is Gerald Durrell. The next person we all should know is the most famous presenter of animal programs, David Attenborough. In the last few years, the craziest and maybe not a particularly good example of a normal Zookeeper is Joe Exotic in the Netflix series *'Tiger King'*. Why? We will go into more details later.

Over the years, we have both observed that zoos are either loved or hated. As Zookeepers being out there amongst the animals, we have often been asked, do you think we should have zoos? Are zoos ethical? The big question is 'zoo versus no zoo'. It's an important question that we have both answered on many occasions. We would like to express our inside view from being committed, dedicated Zookeepers whether we believe in zoos after spending most of our career working in them. This book is a great opportunity for us as two passionate Zookeepers to educate and persuade the public with some good reasons why zoos are important, because not everyone agrees. You will always have people with opinions, but the best opinions are always the ones from those who work in the field and have the inside knowledge. In this case, it's us.

Animals Australia (an animal rights organisation) will debate that 'all animals should be free, you should only see these animals in the wild', or 'just watch them on TV programs.' Now, we support a lot of Animals Australia's views, but this one we certainly question. Healthy debates are always good.

'Born Free'—this phrase is wonderful and even us Zookeepers would agree, but animals in zoos were not born free. It's a great way of thinking, but unfortunately, it's not possible. Even us humans aren't free! Most people are not able to travel and see these animals in the wild, and watching them on TV may not give them the hands-on experience to connect, value and gain empathy for these amazing animals up close. Anything to do with animals will interest us; we always have our ears open. We are pleased to hear confirmation that the impact of zoos on society is largely underestimated by the wider population. This is brilliant because for once this confirms what us Zookeepers already believe in, that yes, zoos are important and have an important purpose.

In 2023, at the University of Exeter in the UK, they conducted research and studies on the impact of zoos on society. *"A zoo is more than a place of entertainment and a collection of animals. Zoos allow us to experience nature and are a great resource for understanding more about conservation, biodiversity and sustainability, bringing many positive benefits to human mental health and wellbeing,"* said Dr Paul Rose, Lecturer at the centre for research in animal behaviour and psychology at the University of Exeter.

This study shows that zoos are a unique and important platform to engage visitors with educational messages which contribute to human health and wellbeing through seeing animals up close. These studies show that zoos appear to have a positive benefit to all species. As a Zookeeper, that is comforting to know.

Another good reason we need zoos is that predation and loss of habit is the big one for animals not being able to live in the wild. Most people are aware that animals are disappearing in the wild, and it's a global problem that we are all responsible for. Here in Australia, ten million hectares have been cleared since 2000, including 3 million hectares of remnant forests, mostly eucalypt woodlands. 7.7 million hectares of this are likely to have been the habitat of threatened species. Many species of animals around the world have disappeared due to loss of habitat in the wild. Sometimes being free means not existing at all thanks to humans' development needs. And they call this progress! Some zoos are doing great work, like breeding for release, where the habitat has been preserved and protected for animal releases. Collaborating with conservation groups is imperative when working in zoos to achieve a positive outcome. I have direct experience in participating in this great work here in Australia, Europe and Africa and value the experience.

All the zoos I have worked at hold their own mission statement for the public to view and it's important to know it as a Zookeeper. A zoo's mission is an individual quote that every zoo has and tries to perform.

For example, the San Diego Zoo in the USA is *'Committed to saving species worldwide by uniting our expertise in wildlife care and conservation science with our dedication to inspiring passion for nature.'*

London Zoo in the UK mission is *'Bringing people closer to nature, inspiring love and care for wildlife at all levels and growing a movement of conservationists.'*

As a Zookeeper, I have tried to remember and understand words that are quoted in this field. Quotes that are used often are important to understand. 'Threatened Species' is one.

These are classified into one of four groups:

- species presumed extinct

- critically endangered (at immediate risk of extinction)

- endangered (at high risk of extinction in the near future)

- and vulnerable (at high risk of extinction in the medium term).

The International Union for Conservation of Nature (IUCN) Red List is important. It is a world list of animals threatened with extinction. In 2024, 41% Amphibians, 26% Mammals, 12% Birds, 37% Sharks and Rays, 36% Reef Corals, 28% Crustaceans, 21% Reptiles and 71% Cycads are threatened.

In my lifetime, zoos have definitely changed and because we all know better now, we can do better. Thankfully this is true in the zoo world. Zoos are an industry, but the cost of running them is extremely high. The majority do not make any profit after paying for all the animals, food, vets, maintenance, enclosures, power, water and staff wages.

Zoos have improved in all ways; they are becoming more sustainable and self-sufficient in many countries. I saw this in my various Zookeeper positions, from having their own free-range chickens, so they can use their own eggs, grow their own fodder, breed their own rats, mice and chicks for food for the animals. The majority of zoos grow their own veggies and fruit as extra supply of food for the animals. Mike and I have been involved in these activities, plus bringing in our own fertile eggs to incubate and hatch for the collection and for food. As part of a Zookeeper on my rounds, breeding mealworms and crickets was also part of my duties, plus bashing drums to get termites out for feed time. These were bought in from the bush for food for a particular species under my care. We have both been involved in encouraging zoos to be more sustainable. Like suggesting and organising a beehive for honey to use for the animals but also to be sold in the shop. At one zoo, I had to collect mosquito larvae from the dam for endangered turtles. Having these items available will help with a good supply of food and keep the food cost down. As you can imagine, the food cost is one of the biggest costs of running a zoo. Whilst working in some zoos, I saw firsthand how bagging up animal poop (Zoo Poo) and selling it for people's gardens was a great benefit. In the UK, customers swear that big cat poo from the zoo put in their domestic garden kept the neighbour's house cat away from their garden! That's pretty cool and recycling at its best.

Another great improvement is that over the years, diets for captive exotic animals have been developed. There are specialised companies around the world that are committed to researching, formulating, validating and producing high quality, consistent animal nutrition for the world's most exotic creatures. Nowadays, you can purchase any stock feed, which is brilliant for everyone because it takes away the stress to supply the correct feed in captivity and prevent sickness and death to specialised animals. Here in Australia, we have specialised food for many marsupials and the correct natural food formulas for birds, mammals and reptiles. Through the zoo network around the world, Zookeepers can get information for the correct food for the animals they hold, with local specialised recipes that have been created. For example, numbats and echidnas eat termites which are collected from the wild for zoos, but we can never find enough, so a substitute egg custard has been developed over the years that is added to their feed. The common but very popular guinea pigs, often kept at zoos, must always have special pellets that contain Vitamin C as they need a high intake of it. So there is no excuse for any animal kept in captivity not to receive the correct food.

Why is history so important to know? If we can prevent past failures, we can continue to improve zoos. Learning from inspiring people like Gerald Durrell, George and Joy Adamson, John Aspinall, Diana Fossey, Jane Goodall and Jack Hanna is valuable. When you are a keen animal lover, like us, you will definitely know these impressive people that started out as either Collectors, Zookeepers or Game Wardens (who also took wild animals for zoos) then became highly respected conservationists from the 1960s.

My favourite program was *Born Free*, the story of Elsa the lion and her life. Unfortunately, it can be a dangerous world, working in countries that may not appreciate conservationists. It was very sad to know that George, Joy and Diana were all tragically killed over the years by being hacked to death in the countries they were working in. The locals did not appreciate their great work which the rest of the world embraced. These mentors encouraged the change of zoos to keep and display animals in captivity differently.

In the UK, the Animals Act 1971 imposed strict liability on keepers of dangerous species for any damage the animal may cause. Then in 1976, the Dangerous Wild Animals Act came in to ensure that where private individuals kept dangerous wild animals, they did so in circumstances where no risk was created to the public and which safeguarded the welfare of the animals.

These Animal Acts helped stop or control animals from being taken from the wild for captivity. One example that has come to light through social media in the last few years is that in 1969, two young Australian travellers who had just arrived in London bought a lion cub from the famous luxury department store, Harrods. I have been to this glamorous department store on many occasions and just cannot picture buying a lion here, but it happened, and these guys said it was an impractical 'impulse' buy. While he was a cub, they felt they could look after him as well as anyone and do their best to secure his future.

These guys were fortunate to find the lion a suitable home (in Kenya, under the care of George Adamson of *Born Free*) as he became too big and dangerous to be kept as a pet. They called him Christian and watching them meet up years later with the lion and embracing him is one of the most touching scenes… animal and human connection never forgotten.

So, in the debate about zoos, as experienced, qualified, skilled and very dedicated Zookeepers, our answer is YES to the question should we have zoos?—but only good zoos with high standards. Please embrace these places fully. They are so important for everyone around the world to experience, resulting in gaining empathy, respect for the animal kingdom and in return to help save species out in the wild.

My Childhood

As I look back, can I say my childhood prepared me to be a Zookeeper? Yes, I believe it did. As a child, growing up in London, I owned a terrapin and a tortoise. My nan in London took me often to the local museum, which had an outside area with some live animals, like Bennett's wallabies to enjoy. I was exposed to a variety of animals when I spent most weekends at my other grandparents' farm a few hours' drive from London out amongst nature. Here I went on country walks with my grandpa and his dogs. He didn't say much, but words were not needed. He pointed out birds' nests, hedgehogs, badger dens and spent valuable time with me, whilst I shadowed him everywhere on the farm. Gran juggled working in the field, running the house, cooking cakes, plucking turkeys. She even raised a fox cub, yes a fox cub as a farmer's wife and so much more. *Yes, I know... here in Oz this wouldn't happen; foxes are not popular here for sure.* My grandparents had a hard but lovely life. Their relationship was loyal, honest and caring with humour. They were a great team. *'That's*

what I want' I thought, and so I was inspired to go out and find it even if it took me to the other side of the world.

As a kid, I loved putting my wellington boots on and getting dirty in the mud in all weathers. But remember, this was the UK, so it was mainly rain, wind and snow! This was my grounding, along with spending lovely summer holidays with my godmother, who had a farm 5 hours' drive from London. These summer holiday visits added to my love for other animals like horses, having my own naughty Shetland pony on loan, hand raising lambs, going to agricultural and horse shows. It felt natural—I belonged in this world, not shopping in London, with crowds, traffic, noise, no space, no nature and no bloody sky.

I was not aware that there were jobs like being a Zookeeper, even when my dad won a building tender and built two large enclosures in two zoos in London, it was not on my radar. I did enjoy zoos though, and as a child, I was lucky to go to work on a couple of occasions whilst my dad built these enclosures for the exotic animals to live in. I certainly would not have thought I'd end up on the other side of the world working in one as a Zookeeper.

As a child, I loved watching TV programs like *Tarzan, Lassie, Black Beauty, Dr Dolittle, Animal Magic* and *Skippy the Bush Kangaroo*. It certainly inspired me to explore the world, and when I reached the age of 18, I went off traveling with my British boyfriend. Australia was my first choice. I was attracted to its enormous wide-open spaces, its massive blue sky, less people, beautiful beaches, the rawness, different landscapes, all the unique animals and carefree attitude. I wanted some of that life. I felt at home in Australia, and it suited my needs. We returned to Australia 3 more times before we made the massive decision to emigrate and live in Australia permanently. Of course, the weather was heaps better than the British weather. Life seemed easier; the UK was changing every day. It was overpopulated, with too much traffic and crime. Australia had not faced this huge challenge back then, but unfortunately now, in 2025, Australia has certainly caught up with the rest of the world. What a real shame for Australia.

As I gained more life skills, I have realized that wherever you live, you think *'the grass is greener on the other side'.* I have been fortunate to live in many places. Wherever you choose to live, there will always be things that you miss from other locations. The best place to settle is where it feeds your soul, so be true to yourself, and Australia was that for me.

Back when I was 14, people didn't really take photos and if they did, it was on a vintage instant Polaroid camera that took amazing high quality photos like this one, well at the time we thought this.

The Magpies Started This Journey

Life can certainly take you in a different direction, just like that. How did I enter the Zoo Kingdom? After a few years of living in Western Australia, I needed a new challenge. It was the WA wildflower season, and my then partner and I decided to visit Kings Park situated almost right in the heart of the City of Perth for a look at the lovely display of wildflowers and stunning trees. As we were enjoying our walk, we found a vulnerable Australian magpie chick on the ground. It was calling amongst the wildflower display. This little chick attracted us to go over and investigate. Both of us stood there watching the chick, looking around for someone to get some advice or help.

The chick's parents didn't appear to be present. Other wild birds were swooping at the chick, stressing the little fella out. I spotted a gardener and ran over to him. The gardener advised us that this was the season for chicks and a common scene. He said some fledglings fell out of their nests and it was best to leave them and hope the parents came back. Otherwise, he suggested taking the chick to a wildlife centre if we were concerned.

Being a little naïve at this time and worried for its survival, we picked up the adorable, iconic magpie chick. It was at this moment my world changed 'big time'. *I had found my new challenge. How could you not have a soft spot for the Australian magpie?*

This was my introduction into the complex world of saving wildlife. When I found this baby magpie, taking it to a Wildlife Rehabilitation Centre was the best thing to do. We wrapped it up in an old t-shirt in a shoe box and telephoned the centre located in the northern suburbs. When we arrived, we were impressed with all the volunteers who were so helpful and the receptionist took our details. We made a donation and luckily, she mentioned that they were always looking for volunteers if I wanted to help out. I felt so excited and instantly filled out the form. Leaving the little magpie felt rewarding, knowing he was going to be helped. The following week, I was volunteering there, meeting some great people and being part of the wildlife warrior team that I proudly felt was my future now.

I found out later that not everyone goes out of their way to rescue wildlife and if some do; they are not always aware that taking any wildlife to a vet or a wildlife centre within 72 hours is the correct way to handle wildlife if found. Maybe the government should help make the public be more aware of their procedures to avoid any confusion and sadness.

My life definitely took a different direction after finding this cheeky magpie chick. This creature changed my world. I became a very active volunteer wildlife carer. I helped out once a week at this wildlife centre for many years, rescuing, caring and rehabilitating all kinds of Australian wildlife. It led me to help out with many magpies, parrots, honeyeaters, with hand raising right up to the ultimate goal of release. In fact, over the years, I have volunteered in many wildlife centres in Australia, the UK, Africa, and Greece. I attended courses and became a registered Wildlife Carer. This gave me the opportunity to hand raise kangaroos and possums for release, which was a dream and an honour. Now I felt a part of Australia.

I found mixing with other people with the same values, being like-minded and participating in volunteering work to be extremely rewarding and great for my well-being. There is nothing better than being part of a team with the same goals, those who love animals and work so hard to save them. It's amazing. The volunteers show such dedication, using the skills they hold, and yes, all in their own time with limited funds. It is so inspiring. Wildlife Centres are run by fundraising and the odd grant. They usually get food donated to them from supermarkets, but unfortunately, the government does not offer much support, even though this wildlife work is so important and necessary.

What we have seen over the years is that hand raising wildlife without the knowledge or skills is a no-go, and only people who are registered as a Wildlife Carer can/should do this. The general public want to help and that's great news, but hand raising and imprinting animals is dangerous and easily done. It's not a good outcome for the animal or the person. There have been lovely stories over the years of similar events, but it has come at a cost. These sweet stories have been turned into books and films and even on the news, but keeping wildlife without the correct licence can cause serious issues and sadness. The government departments can step in and take the animal away, which is devastating. This has recently been brought to light on social media regarding a magpie growing up with two dogs, resulting in a great relationship, but the owners do not have the correct licence to do this, which caused some stress. It can be heartbreaking to make this decision, so the policy is to take any wildlife you find to the nearest vet or wildlife rehabilitation centre, knowing you have taken the correct action, and done well to make the time to rescue the animal. Unfortunately, there is a lot of red tape, compliances and politics, so unless authorisation has been given and the correct licence is held, we advise the general public to not keep wildlife; it's just not worth the headache you will receive. We both feel it's pure bureaucracy at its best here.

Working closely with wildlife carers in the zoo world is part of the lifestyle. My life changed from a volunteer Wildlife Carer to a paid Zookeeper. How did this happen? Well, I was working as a Personal Assistant in an office near the city four days a week. I often had animals under my care from the centre, and I asked my well-presented, young Italian Stallion of a boss if he would consider allowing me to bring in the animals for continued care whilst I was working part time. I explained that the animals would be hidden under my desk, and they were mainly asleep, just needing a bottle, and would not interfere with my office work. Surprisingly, my boss became very supportive of my wildlife rescuing work. In fact, I would chuckle when he showed the joeys to impress potential new girlfriends coming into the office!

Often people would see me carrying my laundry basket with blankets over the top from my car to the office. Even though I tried to do this discreetly, if the two little kangaroo joey heads popped up to have a peek, suited office workers passing by on the streets would be so surprised. Their faces were a picture, and they would comment, 'Wow! You have made my day!' Being involved with the unique Australian wildlife made me realise how little most people know about the animals around them. This was so sad and disappointing, and I hoped things would change, but possibly this observation has just become even worse over the years as humans get caught up in the crazy rat race of living.

Yay, now I am living my life! I wanted to continue in this animal world and improve my skills. So I signed up to attend an Environmental Practice Course at TAFE. On top of working and practicing as a registered wildlife carer, I learnt that if you were studying a relevant course, you could apply to gain work experience at the zoo. I got onto this immediately and sent my expression of interest to the different sections at a local zoo.

I waited with anticipation. This wasn't a shoe-in. I knew zoo work was competitive, but OMG it happened! A Curator called me in for 2 weeks' work experience.

In my head I thought, f**k! I have done it! Even my British de facto at the time was shocked at my persistence, but it paid off. We were jumping with joy. I had managed to break through and get 2 weeks working as a mature trainee Zookeeper through work experience.

Breaking into the zoo world was a unique experience. It was unbelievable, and I felt alive. There was only one other female work experience trainee Zookeeper in my section at the same time. All the Zookeepers were men, but I enjoyed working in this environment. In the men's world, I loved the banter, taking the piss, the simplicity and rawness of the environment they created. I had worked in many industries up to this point; from a PA in a serious office environment, a travel consultant to delivering a fun aerobics class as an instructor. I felt comfortable working in the world of men and enjoyed the atmosphere. It was certainly more straightforward and less bitchy than my previous experiences. It was refreshing. Nowadays, there are a lot more female Zookeepers due to the job being made less physically demanding.

Like many occupations, approximately 30 years ago, all Zookeepers were male. Now in 2025, it appears to have tipped the other way. Either way is not a good thing. You need a balance of males and females in this industry, so let's tip it back a little. We all have different strengths and qualities, and working together is important. I have worked with both, all men and all women, and I definitely like to see a good balance. To be honest, whilst working in the animal field, I have been a little frustrated. I believe, whatever gender you are, if you are doing the same occupation, then all the duties need to be done—that's all duties, no excuses, or leaving the tough jobs for someone else. This pisses other Zookeepers off and is not the correct way to gain respect in your field.

The zoo world was exciting; most days were different, and I appreciated learning. I was in total awe of the magnificent animals around me. Working in a zoo is a physical outdoor position, in all weathers from wind, snow and rain to extreme heat. But working out in the fresh air, learning from other experienced Zookeepers, feeding, cleaning and observing the animals was sensational.

'This is the life,' I thought. Finally, after my journey of searching for a profession I could be proud of, I was making a difference, being a part of the bigger picture and of course finding something that is very important for us all—*to find a job that you are passionate about. (By the way, my office skills were certainly not wasted. I used these skills in the zoo world often, producing reports and much more).*

The Zookeeper's Role

A s animal lovers and Zookeepers, we often say the below quote.

'Working with animals is not your right, it's a privilege, and as a Zookeeper making sure they receive the correct care they deserve is your ultimate aim always.'

Zookeepers are sometimes referred to as an Animal Keeper, Animal Caretaker, Wildlife Park Officer, Zoo Ranger. Let's clear something up, a Zoologist is not a Zookeeper, but more concerned with the research and observation of animals. Zookeepers are trained to work with the animals that live in zoos. In recent years, a large zoo run in the west by the government changed our job title. While the whole world recognises the job title of Zookeeper, they changed it to a 'Technical Officer'. WTF! You can't be serious! What a rubbish name and not recognised for the actual position. What were they thinking? No kid or adult wants to be this, they want to be a Zookeeper.

Around the globe, people recognise the Zookeeper title as someone who manages animals kept in captivity—zoos for conservation or to be displayed to the public. The main duties of a Zookeeper are feeding and daily care of the animals which is called husbandry. But we do not just open the door of an enclosure and throw food at the animals and that's our job done and move on. No one can just walk in and be a Zookeeper for the day, not even if you are an animal lover and have worked with other animals in different fields. Not even another Zookeeper on another section can step in unless you are a trained Zookeeper on this section. It's a welfare issue for the animals and the Zookeepers. No experienced person in this field would disrespect the Zookeeper's position or allow this to happen. This way of thinking is outrageous, but we have certainly had the misfortune of this 'way of thinking' in a poorly managed zoo lacking the knowledge, skills and respect in this area. Giving the keys to an admin person to help out when short staffed has definitely caused us both stress and conflict, which you will see later on in our book. We have found that being passionate and assertive certainly comes at a cost. 'Passionate' is an important word for being a good Zookeeper, and it means a strong feeling of enthusiasm or excitement directed towards an activity or job.

Zookeepers are often seen out in the zoo with buckets, or hosing down, or cycling by with food, but does the general public really know what their role is? Over the years, friends and family, and many others, will say, "Wow! What a cool job being a Zookeeper!" when you start out as a rookie. You will also feel that and be proud. Sadly, after a few years, we realised that while it is a cool job, the humans, red tape and all the politics involved really makes it not so cool and even an unpleasant place to work sometimes.

However, the following facts prove that it is a pretty cool job: One of the first female Zookeepers in New Zealand stayed as a Zookeeper for 44 years. Here in WA a good friend, still a Zookeeper has been doing this for 35 years and was one of the first female Zookeepers in Western Australia.

Zookeepers are responsible for working with captive animals. This means it's our obligation to display the animals in zoos in a way that shows their natural behaviour as much as we can in this zoo environment. We are dedicated to ensuring a positive outcome for all the visitors that hopefully will support zoos for the future.

As Zookeepers, we work hard in preventing 'Stereotypic' or 'Zoochosis' behaviour. Zoochosis is a form of psychosis that develops in animals held captive in zoos. Most often, it manifests in what are called stereotypic behaviors, or stereotypies, which are often monotonous, obsessive, repetitive actions that serve no purpose. Avoiding this is one of the highest duties of a Zookeeper, and great Zookeepers will do whatever it takes to make sure the animals under their care receive the best animal welfare they can. Finding ways to keep your animals stimulated in captivity is a massive priority to us Zookeepers. This prevents unhealthy behaviour and is important for the animals and the visitors.

On many occasions, people have asked us another question, 'How do you become a Zookeeper?' We have given out advice and been mentors to plenty over the years. I have decided to write this book to clarify the understated position of what a Zookeeper does. Zookeepers love all the animals they care for. Yes, it is a dream job to work with animals. We aim to empower all readers with knowing what really happens in this unique

'Zoo World'. It's always interesting to find out more and know what it takes to be a great Zookeeper working in a Zoological Park and hopefully it will surprise you! What we had to learn over the years has been difficult at times, but we want to share the real dirt and bullshit of this world. And of course, all the amazing experiences we have been exposed to on our journey in this unique environment of a zoo.

Back 20-plus years, when I started as a rookie (a trainee Zookeeper here in Australia), I knew no one in this field. There were only scientific books, and none were about the reality of being a Zookeeper. Mike, my partner today, started off around the same time at the same zoo as me, but we never knew each other as we worked on different sections. We only heard each other's names occasionally being called out on the two-ways.

We both say now, with 40 years' experience between us, it would have been very helpful if we'd had the opportunity to get an honest insight into this occupation back at the very start, information contained in a book just like this!

We knew that working with animals is a limited profession—yes, a profession. It's a vocation and a real job and does not just entail standing around all day cuddling animals. As a Zookeeper, you are the voice for the animals and must use it. It's not the time to be quiet as a mouse in this role. Most Zookeepers are fully committed with heaps of natural enthusiasm and should receive good training to put to use.

We both found through our journey there were a lot of highs—some amazing highs—but it can come at a cost, with heaps of frustration and stress, resulting in some very low moments. To add to this, the position of being a Zookeeper and working with animals is not highly regarded for some reason. The pay reflects this, and there appears to be a lack of respect compared to other industries. It's puzzling why, but this appears to be true around the world. Neither of us were prepared for this. Luckily, Zookeepers certainly do not want to be Zookeepers for the pay. We know now that being a Zookeeper is not an easy path to choose, and practicing the three brass monkeys, saying, 'see no evil, hear no evil, speak no evil' is just not possible if you do your job well and put your animals' needs first. Both Mike and I have done this; spoken up when necessary (which has been most of our career.) It's exhausting and comes with stress and problems.

Zookeepers who choose not to do this means the animals under their care will not live their best lives in a zoo. To us, this is not acceptable and very disappointing, but there are plenty who keep quiet and stay under the radar.

All Zookeepers are ambassadors for zoos. The amazing animals on display in zoos, wildlife parks and sanctuaries around the world are the first ambassadors for their species. This allows the general public to get up close and gain empathy for animals and their environment. In our opinion, we would be in a worse situation without zoos. Displaying animals in the best, natural environment is vital for the evolving role of a Zookeeper in a changing world. Experienced Zookeepers should take pride in this, and it will be evident to the visitors at the zoo. Zookeepers need to be inspired in a rapidly expanding industry to undertake vital conservation and animal welfare work as they navigate the changing world we live in. Zoos have evolved over the years, as they should, introducing conservation programs to improve their reputation, which feel good to participate in. Good zoos offer more natural, larger enclosures to create a better habitat for their animals to live in. This encourages the animals to display their natural behaviour and improve physiological wellbeing. Diets are corrected and improved, giving human grade quality food and monitored nutrition. Zoos are no longer just a place to house animals for our entertainment. Organisations like zoos are a safety net for species that may well vanish in the wild. It's therefore necessary to keep species in captivity to protect the ones in the wild.

In our opinion, some zoos or private animal facilities around the world perform great conservation work, but sadly some may use the word 'conservation', but do not fully participate or understand what conservation is. This can be OK, as long as their zoo shows a good example of animals in captivity by educating the public and attracting an audience that will come back to enjoy their experience, taking away a love of animals and their environment. This way, we all have a better chance to coexist with the animals in this world.

We know Zookeepers have definitely inspired many children to become Zookeepers and/or work in the field of conservation. This healthy care for animals helps model good conservation for animal lovers of the future. From a young age, Mike was one of those kids who was inspired to be a Zookeeper and luckily for the animals, Mike finally became a great

Zookeeper and adored his position, showing this through caring and performing his duties at a high standard.

I have noticed in recent years with all the social media coverage that the new Zookeepers need to be reminded more that we all are ambassadors. There are rules about using photos of the zoo's animals on personal Instagram and Facebook posts. As a Zookeeper, we are not there to take selfies of the animals for our own personal profile. If the public sees you do this, it really does not look good and is a safety risk. Most zoos will have a media/marketing department. Hopefully, it's a good one that listens to their Zookeepers, Senior Keepers, Head Keepers and Curators to get the correct information to post. All Zookeepers' photos need to be approved before they go out on your personal media post and often, they will want you to blank out the zoo's logo.

After working in a variety of zoos, I have realised and appreciated that a good media marketing department can make a big difference, keeping the community connected with their local zoo using correct and interesting animal photos and information to draw the public back for another visit. But it is important for the person who is responsible for posting the media items to get their facts correct. Getting the pictures and information approved by the head animal person before it goes public to avoid embarrassing articles is vital, otherwise this will cause unnecessary conflict and jeopardise the reputation for all.

Right from the start of our Zookeeper careers as mature individuals, we both knew it was very important to follow instructions from our experienced Seniors. We both respected this and learnt that we may need to perform a task in spite of any personal emotions or discomfort it brings. We could see it was important that the Zookeeper team needed to work like a 'Bee Hive', and one of the situations that stood out to me in my career was whilst working here in Perth on a captive endangered native species program for release into the wild. I had to experience something that was a little uncomfortable for me.

I was the main Zookeeper for an adorable female marsupial which over the years had been a great ambassador for saving this species in the wild. A numbat is a mammal and the cute emblem for WA. It is a specialised eater of termites, a carnivorous marsupial. This particular numbat had bred many valuable babies for release, but on this occasion, she was dying. She was holding onto her four healthy attached babies that were too small to hand raise at this stage. Each day keeping her alive meant we could save the four endangered babies. The babies needed to get to a certain weight and age under the supervision of the veterinary department. My Senior Zookeeper, Vet department and outside organisations had all agreed to this before we could let the mother rest in peace. Because I was working directly with this animal, it was agonising to watch and be a part of, but it was necessary for me as a Zookeeper to follow the directions that had been agreed on for the sake of the four other endangered babies. It was not my decision to be made. The staff I was under were more experienced and qualified than me, and I needed to follow them.

After a few days, once the babies were at their sustainable age and weight, we could let the mother go, and the vets stepped in. As the Zookeeper, I was then responsible for hand raising these important babies with a

Senior Zookeeper, making sure we kept them wild for release, which we successfully achieved. This particular numbat had been a star.

Working on this section meant I worked with students on research programs. As I was a Research Zookeeper, I mentored university students, supporting them on their research programs through the zoo. These research programs are important for all involved. The information gathered will be used to fund projects to help with local conservation. Some of the results from these studies, (usually Honours, PhDs and Masters) will be presented to the government to gain funding to stop species being wiped out from our environment. We should all be aware that common results show that loss of habitat, climate and predation is the main cause for many species disappearing. Both of us have been involved in a lot of these research programs and find them fascinating, and it's important to get involved with the students and ecologists and participate in their fieldwork. It really helps to understand the species Zookeepers are caring for.

As a Zookeeper working with students and scientists, I found myself not always agreeing with their work. Occasionally there are conflicting agendas between scientists in government research and Zookeepers. As a Senior Zookeeper, Mike had the chance to do some survey work in the northwest of WA at a release spot. This information is collected to keep track of the numbers of marsupials that were released and that have survived. Forty endangered small bilbies (native omnivore marsupials) had been released there, but it was disappointing to find out that a feral cat was responsible for taking approximately 20 of the animals, even though previous feral cat trapping had been done for many years before. Another trapping area was burnt out. There was not one blade of grass left for the animals to take cover in. This was terrible news for us Zookeepers. It left the animals very vulnerable.

Mike asked if the Bilby (a marsupial with big ears used as Australia's emblem for Easter) they trapped in the burnt-out area could be relocated to a better area nearby to give it half a chance. Due to the survey and stats needed, they had to release it where it was trapped. It showed from the trapping that the marsupials were suffering and although the evidence showed that the remaining were in serious trouble; they were left to survive.

It's a sink or swim situation and can be hard to know. Zookeepers may find it difficult to work with scientists who have a different attitude at times.

Another common but often unpleasant duty for some new inexperienced Zookeepers is the need to remove eggs when working with birds. This instruction is necessary if we're not planning to or allowed to breed these birds, or if we are placing endangered bird eggs under a common species to incubate. In these cases, the eggs must be pulled quickly and placed in a freezer. Usually, the fertile egg is not in any stage of development until it has been incubated for a good few days, so removing the eggs as soon as possible is necessary. Whilst working overseas, I had to pull eggs in a breeding program from a common bird and replace it with an endangered bird's egg on a daily basis as part of my duties.

Whilst working as a Flamingo Keeper in Europe, I had to take a flamingo chick off the nest on an island within the flock. I had to do this carefully and whilst holding the chick, another Senior Zookeeper cut its little wing. This is called 'pinning its wing' so it would not fly from the zoo, which has happened in other zoos. The chick would not survive if it escaped to the wild, so it is important, but I did find it horrible assisting with this duty. At the time, I was asking myself, why wasn't the vet performing this procedure? It was a hard learning curve of the job's requirements that certainly made me feel uncomfortable, but it was an instruction and a necessary action to prevent the bird from flying away and being in danger. Deep down, I was not sure I agreed with this action and hoped there may be another way. Note: zoos have certainly moved on, and this experience is not practiced anymore in 2025.

A Day in the Life of a Zookeeper

As a Zookeeper, our daily routine is something like this...

We all arrive a few minutes before we start and go through the staff entrance and sign in to let our Senior in charge know we are on the premises. The same happens at the end of the day. Apart from being courteous, it's a safety issue. A Zookeeper wears a uniform. Some zoos will want you to change into the uniform at the zoo and change out for quarantine purposes. It's pretty amazing, but a lot of animals in zoos do recognise a Zookeeper's uniform.

We then collect our section keys, which are returned at night (in most zoos). Some sections in a zoo have a short meeting every morning with all staff before they start their day so that everyone is aware of what is going on as a team.

It is highlighted in meetings that all Zookeepers are responsible for the animals' welfare, which includes the diets, enclosures, enrichment, animal training, health, capture, restraints and cleaning. As Zookeepers here in Australia, we know we need to consider the five domains whilst performing our duties:

- Nutrition – availability, quality of feed and water

- Environment – atmospheric and environmental conditions

- Health – presence or absence of disease and injury

- Behaviour – restriction or expression of behaviour

- Mental state – In this model, factors considered in the first four domains above cause affective states which are assessed in the fifth domain (mental state). Over time, the objective is to achieve a net balance that favours positive experiences to enable animals to have a life worth living.

Most Zookeepers start around 7.30 am. We always check our animals and enclosures for any damage, including that the electric fence is working, read the handover report, white board and communication diary, grab a two-way, start food prep and go off to service the rounds of animals as trained to do. Communicating well is very important, as things are always changing when you work with animals. It's never a dull moment.

As Zookeepers become more trained in the field, we should be able to look at any enclosure and see what needs to be done to improve it. This awareness should be a natural progression as experience is gained. Rakes and hoses must not be left on show and all feeding bowls should blend into the enclosure and not be placed under perches. All perches and old fodder branches need to be replaced regularly. All poo, sticky food marks need to be removed and hosed down. A good (experienced) Senior Zookeeper, Head Keeper, even the Curator will check the rounds, making sure all Zookeepers are contributing to the workload and keeping up the good standards.

There may be a big cleaning schedule, like dropping a penguin pool to do a complete water change. I was a Penguin Keeper for years. The water is drained, followed by scrubbing and refilling, and this takes time. Wearing protective equipment whilst performing the cleaning is necessary as you may be using chemicals. Animal duty of care is needed to secure them away during the clean. Once it's safe, watching the animals exploring their new clean enclosure is the best feeling, and the animals and the public enjoy this too.

As Zookeepers, we try our best to keep our animals on display for everyone to enjoy, but sometimes it's not possible.

With bigger exhibits and pools, like a seal exhibit, often the Zookeeper needs to get into the pool once the seals are locked away and clean the windows from the inside in the water. Being a Seal Keeper and a Penguin Keeper for many years, I had to perform these duties, and playing in the water was a bonus for me.

There should not be time for Zookeepers to stand around with no jobs to attend to. I certainly have never had a chance to do this. The day goes quickly and there are always more jobs that could have been completed, but as Zookeepers we always need more time in the day.

Most Zookeepers come together for morning tea, cracking jokes, talking about subjects that non-Zookeepers may find distasteful, often grumbling about the sometimes annoying 'public', while they wait for Zookeeper mishaps to record and reveal.

Two-way radios are used by Zookeepers to communicate with each other. Zookeepers often keep to their own section, but the two-way radio is used by every Zookeeper, Vet, Curator, Head Keeper on all sections in the zoo. There are emergency codes that need to be responded to if necessary. Emergency code drills will be practiced a few times a year to cover emergencies, fires, first aid, animal escapes, high risk, low-risk escapes and people entering enclosures. All these codes need to be memorised to follow the instructions, like knowing where safe areas are located, etc. Some Zookeepers will be trained up to be on a Firearms Team. These Zookeepers will be fully aware of how and when to use firearms in high-risk animal escapes. (This is the last resort.) It is courteous to call upon the two-ways to gain permission if a Zookeeper needs to enter another section at the zoo. Zookeepers must always practice health and safety and use a team for heavy work or animal catch ups. They must follow standard operating procedures (SOP) and communicate with the Senior Zookeeper.

Different sections vary depending on the animal's needs. A Zookeeper has to juggle heaps of responsibilities. This may include delivering a keeper talk at a set time and a vet visit to fit in the day, so good planning is necessary. As Zookeepers, we may have to give medication or provide treatment under instructions of the vets.

The Senior Zookeeper may assign particular jobs that need to be completed on top of our normal duties. If animals are already out on display, then they do not need to be let out. Zookeepers need to make sure their animals are on display as much as possible and as visual as they can be for the visitor. If animals are locked away overnight in night quarters, then they need to be let out and their night quarters cleaned. Care must be taken when securing animals to service the enclosures. Primates are a good example of this. During the day, there will be cleaning, washing up, preparing food, and offering enrichment, participating in animal training and refurbishing enclosures, making up the night quarters, catching up animals and health checks.

Part of the Zookeeper's job is to bring in enrichment for the animals like flowers, gumnuts, etc. This can be easy to find on the way to work. There is the Horticulture Department that will often help, but it is down to the Zookeeper to make it happen. Knowing your plants will help with refurbishing and adding enrichment.

You will be working out in all weathers with snow, wind, rain and heat. There is a lot of hosing down and raking up, so knowing how to use some basic equipment is essential. Heaps of maintenance needs to be done like adding new substrate, reperching, mulching, installing new climbing and rope structures, checking enclosures, adding shelters and replacing rat and mice baits. Knowing how to use some tools and machinery is very useful. Zookeepers are required to move 20kgs loads around. This is usually one stock feed bag or a box of frozen fish, etc.

Whilst working with enclosure safety slides, gates, keys and padlocks are very important, and care and concentration are necessary at all times. Securing animals is the highest priority in the Zookeeper's duties. Not securing can be a sackable offense if proven it was from negligence. If animals need to be locked away each night, then often the Zookeeper will be working later times than in other sections. Back in these times, elephants were locked away for the security of the animals and the public, so they needed to stay out as long as possible. Weather conditions are another reason why large animals are locked away.

Zookeepers' duties can vary depending on the time of the year. Different seasons can create different duties. Zookeepers should communicate well and work as a team and help others out when necessary. Animals may be placed in the quarantine area. These animals are serviced at the end of the day under strict instructions. Animals coming into the zoo will be in quarantine for approximately 30 days, depending on the animals and location, and good biosecurity is necessary here.

Zoos are open every day of the year. Some zoos may be closed to the public on Christmas day but Zookeepers work every day as the animals still need to be checked and fed.

Us Zookeepers do not spend much time in the office, (we do not want to) but at the end of the day, we enter details onto the daily report on the computer as an official document of that day. Zoos usually use a Zoological Information Management System (ZIMS). This changes the way you manage, track and analyse data related to the animal kingdom. These include a record of the animals, vet treatment, breeding, transfer, etc. All animals have a Latin (scientific) name that can be quoted. At times, I found it hard to remember these names, but I learnt some of them as I went along, but thankfully most of the time the common name is used.

Zookeepers are responsible for catching up and being ready by restraining the animal for the Vets. All animals that come in and go out of the zoo are run past the Vet Department and the Curators. Health checks and quarantine of animals are necessary for any surplus animals that are being released to other zoos for display or brought into the zoo.

All Zookeepers will be trained up to be involved in animal catch ups, using all different kinds of equipment and techniques. Catching up or restraining animals is always stressful and with risk, but years of skills are put to good use. Most darting of animals is performed by the Head Vet but some Head Zookeepers that are trained can also do this potentially dangerous duty. It is essential for Zookeepers at all levels to listen and work together as a team. Following directions from experienced Senior Zookeepers is highly important to perform this as quickly and safely as possible.

Our Veterinary Friends

When growing up in the UK, I loved reading the funny *It Shouldn't Happen to a Vet* book series by James Herriot. The antics of the animals and the vets were very humorous, leading to watching the TV series, *All Creatures Great and Small*, but apart from that, I didn't have much to do with Vets. But a Zookeeper becomes familiar with these vital members of the team. Most large zoos will have their own Vet Department onsite. This will house experienced qualified veterinary staff that will advise Zookeepers on treatments or ask us to be the handler at the enclosure for the Vet to treat the animals.

A reality check for any Zookeeper is that working in zoos you will always be dealing with animal deaths. Vets and Zookeepers choose when it is right to euthanize, and this is difficult. There are complex ethics surrounding euthanasia, and zoos are always committed to ensuring the best welfare outcome for the animals is species specific. As Zookeepers, it can also be a relief knowing we can perform this as it's not achievable for our loved humans. Zookeepers are often very practical people and understand this situation, though it is always upsetting. When I entered the world of working with animals every day, the biggest adjustment for me was finding a way to accept and cope with animals dying. Mike was more prepared for this as he owned heaps of animals throughout his childhood, but I did find it hard and had to adapt to the practicability of it all.

Most of the animals that die at the zoo will be put into the fridge or frozen and then receive an autopsy. It's an opportunity for education purposes for finding the cause of illness/death for the Vet Department. The first time I walked into the large fridge at the Vet Department in the zoo, it was a little disturbing seeing all sorts of animals just lying there. I wondered what happened to them. I was upset and, to be truthful, a little annoyed when I saw a kangaroo there with a damaged face. I found out later that this kangaroo got spooked and ran into something when the zoo held a night zoo concert event for the public. As Zookeepers we are not keen on these events as we see firsthand from the animals in the zoo the damage these events can do. The noise and lights can be dangerous for the animals' welfare—this type of event is an invasion into their home. It's a classic example of conflict that can develop between Zookeepers and management organising these events. Yes, the zoo needs to raise funds, but night events certainly can cause serious problems that could be avoided.

All deceased animals in the zoo will be classed as a quarantine animal, and a quarantine truck will collect the dead animals for correct disposal. Large animals like elephants and giraffes will be cut up professionally on site to be able to be taken away. This can be difficult to see. Mike expressed to me that he was around when a dead elephant had to be removed in this manner and it's certainly a big downer to experience, but it was all done as respectfully as possible and this is one of the lows you have to deal with.

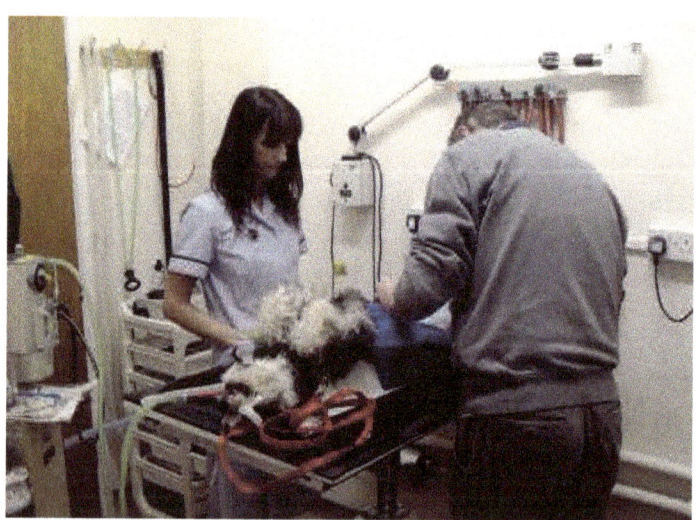

So we now know that Zookeepers work closely with the Vets and Vet nurses, so mutual respect is needed to be shown both ways to allow a good working team for the animal collection. When I worked in a small zoo in the UK and here in Australia, they used a local Vet outside the establishment for their animal care, but this is harder to work with.

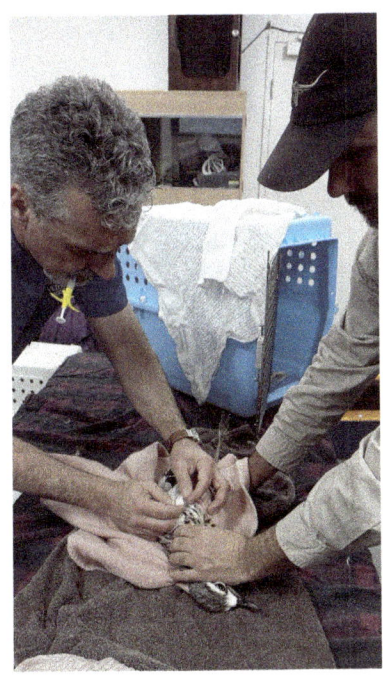

The Vets need the Zookeepers to discuss the animals, including normal behaviour, history and signs, so they can work out the best diagnosis. These Vets may not have as much experience with zoo animals. Getting good medical treatment on hand is so important for the animals and gives confidence to us Zookeepers. It also keeps the high cost down of one of the big expenses of running a zoo and having a good respectful relationship with your Vet is the lifeline of a zoo.

We both are proud that we personally managed to discuss and organise a mutual sponsor with a local vet for a small zoo here in Australia. Before we started, they were randomly going to any vet, so there was no consistency. We negotiated with this local vet who became our sponsor vet for the zoo. He held wildlife experience here and abroad, including Africa, and has great skills in all

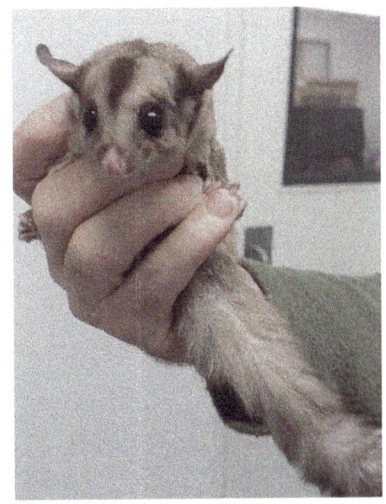

areas. It was a massive benefit, offering great vet health care to the animals in this small zoo. For Zookeepers, this is highly important for the animals under our care. This good vet is also one of our personal vets for our 150 animals on our rural property, so we can relax, respecting his skills and knowledge.

 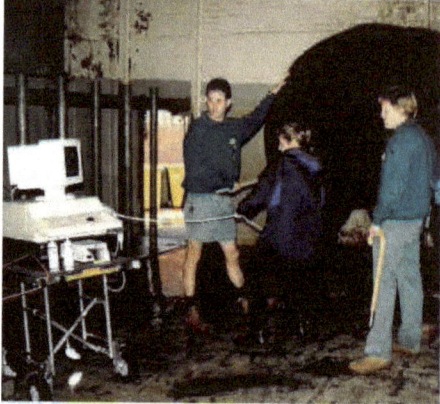

Mike helping zoo vets with the procedure of checking the elephant's fertility status.

Now a Zookeeper

Now I had achieved the title of Zookeeper, (well, a Rookie 25 years ago) in the Bird Section, I had to earn it. This meant being trained and learning from other skilled Zookeepers. It's an apprenticeship; you do not become a respected Zookeeper overnight. I soon realized that I was a glorified cleaning person most of the time. It's true, but it's important to know what the real job entails.

Every day I was like a sponge. I could not get enough of it. My Curator at the time said, 'I was a breath of fresh air, and I fitted in well.' I had no idea what it was like to be a Zookeeper behind the scenes, but I felt so proud to have the opportunity to be there. Every day, I went home so tired I could hardly eat. I wore big heavy boots and was on the go all day. I felt mentally and physically exhausted.

My position as a bird keeper ranged from providing the correct habitat and approved diet for a lot of species of birds. In fact, here in Australia there are around 850 species of birds. 45% of them aren't found anywhere else, so as a bird lover, it's a great place to gain your avian kicks. I was very happy working with these birds. I had to have great observation skills, working with the delicate blue wren to the distinctive black cockatoo to the dangerous cassowary. I became one of the main penguin keepers, which led me to other opportunities in my career overseas. Whilst I was working with one of the smallest animals in the zoo, my future partner Mike was working with one of the biggest animals in the same zoo.

After two weeks of my amazing work experience, I knew that I would have to make some decisions in the near future to gain a more secure position at a zoo. I continued for a week with my PA office position, but then I received an unexpected phone call, offering me a one-month casual Zookeeper position on contract at the zoo.

Gosh, gaining work as a Zookeeper in a zoo was like gaining my first puppy, just an unforgettable experience, one of the best highs.

Wow! Now I needed to take a chance and do it, but it was a gamble—a gamble I was so glad I made. I handed in notice for my office PA position and took the chance. Sometimes you have to take a calculated risk.

This one-month contract as a Zookeeper on the Bird Section turned into years of being on a long contract, experiencing different sections in the zoo and allowing me to complete my Zookeeper Certificate III. At this stage, the zoo paid for my course until my contract expired. The race was on to complete it, which I achieved post haste.

Juggling study, some wildlife caring and working full time was not easy, but I was so motivated and excited. The competition within the zoo industry is bloody high. There were many other casual Zookeepers around the zoo who wanted the same jobs.

We were all on contract at the zoo and all trying to stay high on the pool list for the next contract that came up. It was obvious that to succeed, I needed to be available and keen to grab any offer at any time. Those who stood out and got the offers had to be self-motivated and a good team player, which I naturally was.

When Zookeepers socialize together, we are a right mixture of people, generally a motley crew, not always politically correct, and at times, we could be called vulgar. Zookeepers will talk about animals, incidents and weird stuff like the size of a gorilla's penis. Not the usual office conversation, which is often about kids, schools and the best coffee—certainly not about penis size, but Zookeepers do! On this particular social evening, a Primate Keeper spoke up about ape penis sizes compared to human size. I laughed at the time. I couldn't believe we were talking about this. I thought they were having a 'giraffe' (that's a laugh) with this. After a few more beers, the story got more involved, getting into penis size and anthropomorphism, comparing them to the humans who are often claimed to have the largest penises among primates. Wow! The facts were true for penile girth, but not for length, given that chimpanzee and bonobo erect penis length is comparable to that of humans. By then, the Primate Keepers had pulled together and started to tell us all that a male chimpanzee has a similar size to a human and weighs around 60kgs and stands around 4 feet tall and can lift around 200kgs of dead weight. Male orangutans have smaller penises and weigh approximately 100kg and stand around 4 feet tall and can lift up to 800kg of dead weight. Then male gorillas have even smaller penises compared in size of the chimpanzee and orangutan. A large male silverback gorilla weighs 195kg and stands around 5 feet tall and can lift over 800kg of dead weight. It was fascinating, and we all learnt much on the subject that night.

Whilst we were talking about primates, I brought up my experience of primates whilst overseas that were behaving badly towards me. It was all tongue in cheek, and it allowed everyone to crack jokes whilst I told them what happened to me whilst working in the Channel Islands. As Zookeepers, we love our animals and are very dedicated to them, but sometimes it's like being a parent—we do not always receive the same love back. As Zookeepers have all been pissed on, spat on and much more, we should not take it personally and I do not. One moment that stands out for me was when I entered the safety raceway of some apes; a bachelor troop of gorillas in their night quarters when I visited the male Zookeeper responsible for this bachelor group. The male gorillas instantly started to flirt with me, flashing their eyes at me, being vocal and trying to catch my attention a little intimidatingly, I must say. I followed the health and safety instructions and kept my distance from the gorillas, but it was amusing to see them flirt. I had never received so much attention!

Another ape encounter was with a congress of female orangutans. This time, it was not so nice. They all spat at me and kept on spitting. Apparently, they did not like the competition of a female Zookeeper entering the night quarters with their male Zookeeper. It was their way of showing jealousy and telling me to 'bugger off'.

The other funny situation was with a very large male silverback gorilla from Melbourne Zoo, which was on loan to this zoo in the Channel Island in the UK, where I was working. Most mornings, I would walk past this magnificent creature whilst he was out on display sunning himself, but once he spotted me, he would rise up and start to thump his chest. He then would continue to let out a musty BO odour, charge around being vocal and continued to do this most days I passed him. The people who watched it would laugh, enjoy and find amusing the display, whereas I was always trying to pass this silverback discreetly to avoid this spectacular display of affection. One primate keeper said, maybe he knows there is a fellow Aussie around? We all had a giggle.

Then I met some naughty parrots that were handed over to a zoo in the UK. They were donated from a pub because of their bad language which might have been offensive but certainly attracted many customers to visit this zoo. These parrots made the visitors laugh and helped people recognise the birds' intelligence and beauty through a fun experience. We love parrots and agreed it was a great attraction and we would visit this zoo to see them. Sadly, some people still complained about their vocabulary even though the zoo had warning signs up and displayed them in a suitable area. Unfortunately, political correctness is even spreading into the animal world!

Zookeepers do not socialize often but when we do, it's pretty wild, and there's always a Zookeeper hand raising some animal for the zoo. Listening to other Zookeepers' experiences never gets boring, it's always stimulating. The conversation with about 30 Zookeepers can be loud and interesting.

After some banter with each other on the best animals to be looking after as Zookeepers, the subject of male animals being good fathers arose. It was interesting with all contributing to the subject. Some species are proud fathers that play an integral role in raising the young with, or sometimes in place of, the mother. The Australian emu is a unique animal in that they have male-only parental care, which is only true for about two percent of bird species. Tending the nest is a huge investment for an emu dad. He rarely eats or drinks during this time and can lose up to half his body weight. Once the female lays the eggs, she will abandon them, and the male will incubate them for up to eight weeks. Emu chicks stick closely to dad for up to six months. Seahorses and their close relative, sea dragons, are the only species in which the male gets pregnant and gives birth. Male seahorses and sea dragons get pregnant and bear young, a unique adaptation in the animal kingdom, and they are pretty adorable and very relaxing to watch.

In this particular conversation, all the Zookeepers were butting in with their thoughts. They brought up a few other male animals which have a massive input in fatherhood, including Emperor Penguins, Marmosets Monkeys, Mountain Gorillas and the Arctic Wolf. For once, the male Zookeepers all looked very proud of themselves when quoting this information to the loud female Zookeepers teasing them.

Despite the banter, zoos often hold hostile working environments which create unpleasant practices amongst other Zookeepers. It was very disappointing to witness how low some people will go to gain their Zookeeper position. It soon became clear that our only friends were the animals. The politics in zoos (which management created) was one big pile of bullshit, and there was a lot of monkey business going on in this jungle.

We knew we could trust the animals, but unfortunately loyalty is not always shown in the human race, and trust will be broken when working in this environment. This was hard to adjust to, but the fact is, for every Zookeeper position, hundreds of people apply for it, and the situation has been like this for many years. It needs to change, but I couldn't see it happening soon, especially in Australia with such limited positions.

Mike Now a Zookeeper

Mike started around the same time as a Rookie Zookeeper, but in the Elephant Section, finding his dream job as a Zookeeper later on in his career. He had been working as a dog handler in the army and as a truck driver on the mines.

Mike is a born and bred Western Australian who loved the zoo and visited it often when growing up. He knew all his life that he needed to work with animals to feel complete for himself, but mainly for the love and welfare of animals. In fact, he owned his first guinea pig when he was just 4 years old. At this time Mike had a family and gave up a decently paid job to relocate back to the city, hoping he could find a Zookeeper position. Mike had his own 5-acre hobby farm and every opportunity that came up, he applied for vacant positions at the zoo. He eventually got his perfect job in a unique animal section, working hands on with one of the most popular but dangerous animals in captivity—the majestic Asian elephant. Mike said he felt so alive when he got this position.

Mike was trained as a police dog handler in the army, to be the security on army aviation base. These dogs were trained to detect and possibly attack intruders. There were only 10 other soldiers trained in this sort of dog handling in the army, with the dogs trained to police dog standard at a RAAF base in Queensland. These dogs were security dogs for the military base and worked closely with the soldier. These skills helped Mike gain his position as an Elephant Handler (Zookeeper) in a WA zoo. Mike was fortunate to own heaps of pet animals over his life and had gained empathy and great skills with the responsibility of caring for them. Owning his own pets gave him the best grounding and put him miles ahead.

Whilst we were both following our hearts and our own journey to be great Zookeepers, little did we know we would eventually join up around 10 years later when I returned from being overseas for some time.

Mike was following the same path as mine but stayed in one place, here in Australia, working with different animals to me. We had a similar background; he was a registered Wildlife Carer, attending the weekend DBCA course before he became a Zookeeper and continued to help wildlife whilst working full-time as a Zookeeper. He was helping out where he could and rehabilitated many magpies for the same wildlife rehabilitation centre as I did. Mike concentrated on the northern suburbs and me the southern suburbs, so our paths never crossed. But we both have a love for the Australian Magpie and always will.

Working with elephants is a specialised and hands-on section. You get up close with your animals every day. It's both physically and mentally demanding, as there's a lot of daily animal training to practice. Consistency is a must for the wellbeing of the elephants.

Whilst working on the elephant section, Mike was super keen and grabbed extra duties when he could to gain more skills. He experienced working with the Serval cat and the aviary of African birds, often during his lunch break.

He was also one of five Zookeepers trained and allowed to enter the hand-raised cheetah enclosure to provide stimulation but also hands on physical inspections. Mike was lucky enough to advance his skills by assisting on other megafauna sections, such as the giraffe and rhino areas.

Like me, Mike started his career at the bottom, working his way up to the Head Elephant Keeper, and after 9 years, transferred to the Australian Section for another 8 years as a Senior Zookeeper, eventually running the Nocturnal House. Mike's passion, dedication and drive shows every day. This makes him a great mentor to have around. He always delivered great animal husbandry, showing never-ending motivation, energy, and devotion for his Zookeeper position.

We have learnt on this journey it goes a long way as a trainee Zookeeper to be keen and learn some basic facts of this field and the animals you are caring for. It's crucial for all Zookeepers to keep up to date, read articles and ask other experienced people in the field. A good Zookeeper is open to a lifetime of learning and that means learning from practical experience, not just reading a blog on the internet and treating it as gospel and quoting it. Mike and I have a big list of contacts that we value and use to learn more from if needed. We receive calls too. Leaving a university with a degree is great, but it doesn't mean you are qualified to be a Zookeeper. Some new Zookeepers walk in thinking they go straight to the Senior Zookeeper and jump five years forward. How wrong they are, and this attitude is not just limited to the zoo world. I have heard from friends in other animal fields, like vet nurses who experience this same problem, likewise on farms and in stables. The saying 'learn to walk before you run' is appropriate here. With all our experience, we both agree on what makes a great Zookeeper—training, training and more training by experienced mentors. Exemplary Zookeepers have natural talent, and with training and experience become invaluable Zookeepers. Good mentors are the only way to become a great Zookeeper, you cannot do this alone.

Mike has often said that what we should have in common as great Zookeepers, is that we think the animals we look after are the best. *Just like we always think we have the best dog in the world.*

The dedication shown by most Zookeepers is hard for non-animal people to understand, and bosses can take advantage of their commitment at times. Mike told me of a funny situation he was put in, because he was so dedicated to the animals under his care. It was a matter of *'chains or shit yourself'* for him.

As we all should know, elephants were one of the most dangerous animals to work with in captivity. Intelligence, size and strength is a potential threat on a daily basis. They are emotional and can be anxious and get spooked with loud noises which they can hear from long distances. Elephants certainly react to unknown things, so to prevent them from hurting themselves or Zookeepers and public, they were one of the animals that are locked away in the barn each night.

The general public may not be aware of this, but it's not uncommon to restrain elephants by chains around their feet for feeding or vet treatment. During Mike's early years on the Elephant Section, and waiting for the upgrade of the exhibit, these elephants were chained overnight in a barn. We all agree this is not an ideal situation for an animal that only sleeps 4 hours a night. As a dedicated Zookeeper, you want your animals to have full movement to explore freely as long as they can, so these animals are one of the last animals to be put away each night and probably one of the last Zookeepers to go home.

This particular morning, Mike woke up to find his wife and two kids very sick with gastro. Mike felt a bit off, but OK, and there was no way he could not go to work as there was a shortage of qualified, experienced elephant keepers at that time (a safety requirement was two Zookeeper policy at all times with the elephants).

Not going into work meant leaving the elephants on chains all day away from the public, and this was not an option for Mike. He was almost at the zoo when...*oh no*, the gastro kicked in. His gut followed through and 'sharted' (that's a nasty combination of farting and sh..tting!) his jocks.

WTF! Mike had no option but to quickly pull over, to rip his jocks off, bag them and throw them into a park bin. He rushed to his locker at the zoo, had a shower, changed his uniform and continued his 10-hour shift working with these majestic animals. When working with animals, you will understand the decision he made. It's always about the animals and the best you can do. *He certainly was not in the good books with his wife and children when he returned home that night, but as long as the elephants were happy, that is all that matters!*

As Mike was gaining a relationship with the four elephants, he found exchanging ideas, skills and having someone come to your zoo for hands-on specialised training for any level Zookeeper is a massive bonus. These Zookeepers are not treading on anyone's toes, and there is no need to feel insecure. To be a better Zookeeper, it's necessary to be open to learn from others that may have more knowledge in this area. Even as experienced Zookeepers, Mike embraced this and was grateful to gain experience from an Elephant Keeper native to Asia who travelled with the elephants to Australia. This Elephant handler had worked with these giants all his life.

Then an American Elephant Keeper who handled many elephants at one time in captivity stayed and worked with him. A British elephant handler who had a great reputation with good elephant training in zoos dropped into the section for a while, too. When Mike took over the Head Elephant

Handler position on the Elephant Section here in WA, he requested management to participate in a paid zoo trip to the Eastern States to visit other zoos' elephant programmes. At this time, there were only 7 other elephants in Australia. Meeting up with other Zookeepers, discussing and sharing ideas is very important and necessary, and Mike brought back ideas, including the use of frozen bran blocks for the elephant, which is still being used at the zoo.

Mike knew that after a few years of working on the Elephant Section, he had built up a good relationship with the four elephants and became dedicated to their needs.

It's an Amazing Job

Yes, it's an amazing job, but it takes time to build a good relationship with animals, especially when working with megafauna like primates, elephants and big cats. A Zookeeper needs to offer consistency to keep the animal and humans happy and safe at all times. Some of these duties will be daily training to gain this mutual respect. Some zoos will display the animal training for the public to view, others perform the training off display, which is a shame.

Let's start with some colour, some pink glamour! Whilst working overseas, I noticed most zoos have a flamboyance of flamingos at the front entrance, making an eye-catching scene when you enter. They are popular animals to watch around the world. People love these long-legged pink birds. It's all about the colour and these are usually the first exhibits you see when you walk into the zoo outside of Australia. Unfortunately, it's not possible to import flamingos into Australia—not even by egg to incubate or raise, which is a real shame. This is due to outdated laws in Australia and New Zealand.

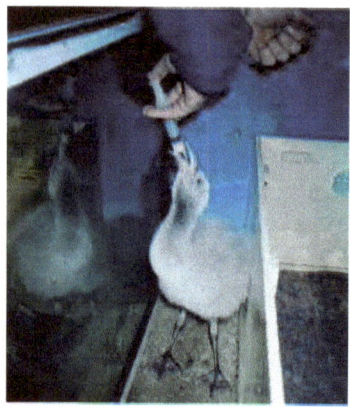 

I was lucky to be a Zookeeper for a large flock of around 50 of these colourful birds in two zoos in the UK. They eat special food pellets with crustaceans added to it, and they filter their food in the water, making plenty of noise. Their legs look fragile, and yes, if they are in colder climates, they are kept in sheds with heaters overnight. Every morning, I had to crack the ice on the lake and clear any ice on their paths so the flamingos would not slip and damage their long legs.

Having the opportunity to raise a flamingo chick was lovely... Well, apart from the blended fish smoothie I had to make and syringe in each morning! I would often be covered in this stinky stuff. I walked the chick back to the flock each morning, and each night walked it back to its warm night quarters. Eventually, once big enough with its full plumage, the young flamingo stayed with the flock all the time and enjoyed eating the special floating pellets that contain the crustacean formula, which helps keep the vibrant colour of the plumage we all adore.

As a Zookeeper, we are always excited to see the animals we look after in zoos out in the wild. This happened a few years later whilst I was having a break from working in zoos. I held a normal office position in a large travel company in the UK, but needed my animal fix, so I participated in some wonderful penguin rescue, rehabilitation, and conservation work in South Africa. It was here that I was lucky to see wild flamingos on a lake. They flew above me, which was wonderful to witness, a real bonus.

Conservation

As Zookeepers, we are often aware of some terrible conservation disasters, bad animal welfare situations and cruelty out there in the big bad wide world. We represent ourselves as animal lovers and conservationists and so should be out there mucking in by getting involved in local conservation projects. We have both attended either on our own or together with community action groups, saving animals and promoting conservation. It is important that Zookeepers are aware and support these groups. They need all our support and are great learning opportunities. For a passionate Zookeeper, this voluntary work takes no effort to be part of, it's a necessity. We have attended many of these events—tree planting, nesting boxes placement, surveys, tracking turtles, cockatoo counts and many endangered marsupial surveys. It's rewarding and highly recommended. We find it exciting, but maybe it's just us who feel this way! In addition, as Zookeepers we can offer our skills and give the projects credibility which in return will possibly gain more awareness resulting in gaining support and private funding, or government and local authority grants to improve this situation.

One of our biggest battles is finding suitable habitat for release. The critically endangered WA ringtail possums are constantly being pushed out of their habitat from development in the southwest of WA. Wildlife Carers are working hard to rescue or hand raise these adorable creatures. Finding suitable spots to release back into a safe and good environment is always the issue. Making sure there are good release spots is vital to prevent all the good work of saving the species in captivity being undone. Unfortunately, the government does not always listen or show respect. They uphold out-of-date decisions. People doing this difficult job are not always in agreement either, and working together to understand both sides and what is best for the animals is always the top priority, but it can cause heated discussions and conflict. Both of us say it shouldn't be about statistics for the government, but sadly it can be.

Whilst working as a Zookeeper (Research Zookeeper), I was directly involved with a Species Recovery Plan for a range of native WA animals. In a zoo, every animal is crucial to the breeding program. On this program, thousands of animals have been bred and released into protected wild habitat to help secure a future for these species. Working on the native breeding section allowed me to advance my skills by being involved in everything, including swabbing, using microscopes, checking fertility, genetics and pairing, to the collaring and release of the babies. I was the main predator trainer with a live bird of prey for an endangered native animal that was performed prior to their release.

Using the falconry skills I gained whilst working overseas became very useful on my return. Predator training involved taking a bird of prey out on the glove into the enclosure to encourage the 'take flight and run into a tunnel' action when they saw or felt one of their main predators in the wild, which is usually a raptor (bird of prey) like a hawk or eagle.

Not all conservation work is easy. The next story is a sad one to tell. It was a horrible occasion for me. The victim was a valuable endangered mother numbat nesting in a log with her four babies. One of the babies was dead. We found the culprit, a rat nest under the endangered animals' nesting log. The baby had been bitten by a rat and died. This issue was dealt with immediately as we could have lost four endangered numbats if the feral pest was not eradicated. There is nothing worse on the conscience of the Zookeeper if this is not done efficiently. Some zoos have issues with wild birds, like seagulls and pigeons. These birds also need to be trapped as they eat the zoo animals' food and spread disease, thus threatening the zoo collection.

Zookeepers around the world work with biologists, ecologists, and conservationists to make a difference with in situ breeding and taking part in research and conservation. Each country has their own endangered species problems, and some animals are down to their last few numbers, but many have been increased in zoos and released back into the wild. Some of these animals were even listed as extinct but were rediscovered, which is very exciting news to everyone. Back from the brink of extinction is amazing.

I was directly involved in two of these success stories whilst working as a Zookeeper. This certainly highlights the value of the position of a Zookeeper.

- Native Black Rhinos in Africa that are critically endangered are being helped by humans doing whatever they can to protect them from being made extinct with the world watching.

- In the USA, the Black-Footed Ferret was on the brink of extinction but captive breeding for these mammals has saved these creatures.

- In the UK, the Red-Billed Chough bird was once classed as extinct, but due to captive breeding and reintroduction, people have seen these birds back in the wild.

- In Mauritius, the Pink Pigeon was on the edge of extinction and has been bred and reintroduced into the wild.

- In Western Australia, the Western Swamp Tortoise was classed as extinct for 100 years. In 1953, they were discovered in the wild. These tortoises have been bred and reintroduced into the wild now to keep the numbers up. Zoos working with conservation groups certainly shows the important work that is being achieved.

One that interests Mike and myself is the thylacine. Commonly known as the Tasmanian tiger, it is a carnivorous marsupial native to Australia and Papua New Guinea. Media coverage is saying it's *out there we just need to find it and save it.* In 1936, it was classed as extinct and scientists want to bring back the Tasmanian tiger from so-called extinction. They say they can by genetic engineering techniques to edit the DNA of a closely related species. In recent years, it's reported to have been now classed as an **extant animal** (meaning still in existence but surviving). Recent studies with biologists out in the field in Papua New Guinea and Australia have brought to light signs and evidence that the thylacine may still be out there living in remote areas, so let's hope that in a few years we will all get to experience the sighting of a live thylacine not a taxidermy exhibit.

Activists

Let's talk about Animal Activists. Are they friends or foe for us Zookeepers?

Animal activists can do some great work and are needed as the last resort, but they can also be a real problem with their extreme animal rights opinions, which can actually jeopardize some animal welfare. Their behaviour can be over the top, causing unnecessary issues from lack of knowledge in this field.

One well-known organisation is PETA (People for the Ethical Treatment of Animals), dedicated to establishing and protecting the rights of all animals around the world and has done some great work, like shutting down poor animal welfare facilities.

From experience, some Animal Activists can do some damage with their reckless actions. It was too much for me to witness when I got caught up in some protesting whilst I was driving down a country lane in the UK. My friend was in the passenger seat, and I was following a big black van that took up most of the country lane. I suddenly heard the fox and hound trumpet, dogs were barking, horses with their riders in pink jackets (they are actually red) were everywhere. Suddenly the black van stopped, the doors opened, and heaps of people in black balaclavas and battens jumped out.

It was terrifying. I told my friend to lock her door. We couldn't go anywhere, so we watched. These people attacked the horses and tried to pull off the riders. It was disgusting. I shouted at them, "You arseholes, you are supposed to be 'animal lovers', stop hitting the horse!" The riders and dogs got away, and all the activists jumped back into the van and raced off. It was a horrible experience.

I see both sides. I understand that the death of a fox in this manner may not be humane by being chased by lots of riders on horses and then ripped apart by hounds. But acting like this as an animal rights activist by hitting horses and being aggressive is not the answer and shocking to see. Two wrongs do not make a right.

We should all be aware that we are not just Zookeepers; we represent the highest care for animals. We are Wildlife Advocates and naturally display this by buying free-range eggs and free-range meat and participating in getting better animal welfare in all areas. On my days off for many years, I would volunteer at a Black Cockatoo Rehabilitation Centre. I'm not sure how I fitted it all in, really! But this was so fulfilling, getting up close to these amazing, endangered birds and being involved to save and get them back into the wild.

For the love of the unique large Black Cockatoos, I spent a lot of my time being active—performing education talks, bird training, fund raising, picking up sick, injured black cockatoos from vets and taking these birds to the zoo for treatment before they were taken to the centre for a long process of rehabilitation for release.

There are so many animal organisations that need our zoo keeping skills, and many of us offer our assistance and are an active part of the bigger picture where possible. Most of us do join Animal Welfare organisations, make donations, sign petitions and much more. It's our lifestyle to be proactive where we can.

Cameras On, Zookeepers Bring a Zoo Back from Extinction

Whilst working in the UK on an organic farm, a Senior Zookeeper I worked with years prior in a Zoo in the Channel Islands made contact with me via Facebook. I gave the ex-gorilla keeper a call, and he had a job opportunity for me that sounded more than interesting. Apparently, a private zoo had been closed down in a lovely part of the country in the UK. PETA managed to get this run-down zoo shut down because it offered poor conditions for the animals in their collection. I understood they took videos and photos and exposed the privately run zoo, which had deteriorated over the years. The local authority then advised the zoo to shut down and took away their special zoo licence until a solution could be considered in the future.

This private zoo had then been sold to a family that had no experience in running a zoo. My friend was the new Curator, and he was looking for a good team of experienced Zookeepers to support him on this big task and wanted me to join the team.

I understand that these conditions were not acceptable and the people that were involved in this movement had good reasons to highlight it, but they may not have been aware that the animals involved—bears, tigers, lions, monkeys—were in danger of being put down if new homes in other zoos were not found and the zoo was shut down. These animals would become surplus animals in the zoo world. If the animal had no genetic value, or were too old, some of them would be euthanised. I was made aware that many of the animals did not hold any genetic value to support breeding programs in other zoos.

Thankfully, the previous Zookeepers working there felt strongly to protect the animals and worked for free to keep the animals alive whilst this situation was being resolved. The original Zookeepers did not want to leave the animals, so they lived on site and struggled to find enough food to feed the animals. They did not get paid, and it was a very stressful time for them all, but I totally understand why. Luckily, most of these Zookeepers stayed on under the new Curator.

I was one of the new four qualified, experienced Zookeepers that was part of the regulations for the zoo under new Curator/Owners. The new owner had never worked or owned a zoo and to be honest a bit of a 'muppet' for us experienced animal staff to deal with.

It was clear that on his own he did not have the experience, qualifications, knowledge or skills to get the zoo reopened to the public again. It was pleasing to know when these restrictions compelled the owner to employ four qualified experienced Zookeepers. Three of us were Zookeepers in the Channel Islands and the last Zookeeper was a big cat Zookeeper that came highly regarded. The Curator of the zoo had a massive mission to get it up and running to be safe for the animals, staff and visitors. He had full support with us, and we worked hard and well as a team.

This zoo became famous when the film '*We Bought a Zoo*', (yes, with Matt Damon!) came out a few years ago and was based on this zoo in Devon, England. The film told the story of this zoo being shut down and reopened.

However, this Hollywood feel-good film was not really the true version of what happened at the zoo. I know, I was there; it was based very thinly on it and portraying it as a cute and cosy situation which it was far from. The film certainly did not show our frustration with the lack of understanding from the new owner.

Apart from the huge job of improving the animal welfare, to add to the Curator and Zookeepers' difficult job, the new owner was very much into the media. He was a journalist (a talker) and wanted to make sure his story was covered at all times. A reality TV series was set up whilst we were trying to achieve this big task. The Curator, who was a friend, had many sleepless nights with fears of lions and tigers getting out *(which they did...)*.

He had good reason for having these nightmares. Most of the enclosures were falling down, the fences rotten, no money, no food, or good vet treatment, etc. The four of us pulled together all our knowledge and contacts from other zoos and worked well together for the 8 months to turn it around. Unfortunately, there were many heated moments with the owner (a non-animal person) with us experienced Zookeepers. The owner really had no idea about the requirements of this animal world, causing frustration and conflict most of the time. A few times the TV crew had to stop filming whilst we got it together and fisty cuffs were dropped. *It was looking like a real cat fight!*

The day the Curator, the local shire and the Zoo Inspector signed this zoo to be fit for opening was a massive achievement for us. All the animal and ground staff should be proud, knowing what mega achievement it was. The owner really did not understand, value or appreciate the massive effort it took from the four of us to get his zoo back up and running, but that's life, hey.

It's so good to know that our effort was not in vain; the zoo was renamed and is presently going very well and has over 80,000 visitors a year. It's well known in the UK from the TV series, book and film. It's now a charity-based zoo, and it's great to see that all our hard work at the beginning has not been for nothing. Even though soon after the zoo was reopened, we all went our own ways in the animal field. I still keep in contact with the three Zookeepers. We certainly delivered what we aimed to do, and everyone is now enjoying and benefitting, most importantly all the animals.

I remember that being filmed all day is no holiday. Having the big responsibility of making this zoo safe for the animals, Zookeepers and the public, raising the standards and displaying the animals in great habitats was a big ask. But the bigger task was having a bloody camera crew present whilst we were getting the licence back to reopen the zoo; it was no joke. The TV crew were filming the whole process, making it into a reality TV series. We were not given an option to not be included in this filming, and having a camera crew following us around all the time was an added nuisance. Simple things like going to the toilet and not turning the mic off turned out to be embarrassing when the whole camera crew heard me spending a penny! The teasing I received was relentless. When the show went live in the UK, people started to recognise me at the shops, and it was all unwanted attention. In fact, being part of a reality show is not much fun. The camera crew waits for someone to lose it to show some excitement in a reaction or conflict. Certainly, this was the place to find it. Then when the series comes out and you watch it to find it's been edited and taken out of context, it can embarrass you.

By the time the show was released, I had left the zoo and was now an Operational Manager Assistant for a luxury holiday home business. I supervised 13 people in the office and the next day they had all seen the show. Luckily they all liked it, but my new boss had a few comments and I had to explain the different life working in the zoo world so he could understand that I had to kick arse sometimes to achieve things. It was a little awkward that morning, but I appeared to be popular with the rest of the office workers!

Feeding the Animals

Let's talk about food. There is no time for vegans in the zoo world, that's what we say! People who love animals do not always realise that you may have to provide other dead animals for them. All animals have to be fed with the correct food, and that is often other cute animals.

As a Zookeeper you will have to do this, and I would like to mention it's OK to be a vegan as a Zookeeper, but your opinion should not affect performance. Over recent years, the zoo industry has attracted more vegan Zookeepers which is fine, but it's often a Zookeeper's duty to chop up dead animals to feed out. This also means gassing animals humanely like chicks, mice and rats for food or for pest control. If gas is not available, the Zookeeper may have to kill humanely in a way that has been approved by the ethics' committee. That doesn't happen often, but Zookeepers will be trained to do so in case of an emergency. Like most people, I found it upsetting the first time I had to gas chicks, rats or mice, but it is a necessity and does become a little easier with time. Working in a variety of zoos, I have found that some have their own breeding program to feed out to the collection of animals. Others will get the food delivered, dead and frozen. Nothing gets fed out live. That's illegal—only crickets and mealworms can be fed live. Feeding snakes with dead rats, mice, etc. whilst the visitors watch on can be hard to perform at first, but the visitors appear to find it interesting, and often I had to do this, though it wasn't my favourite job.

Whilst overseas working in the UK, I had the opportunity to work at a friend's Birds of Prey Centre. In Europe, it's a very popular pastime, and it's common to own a pet owl, falcon or hawk. There is a lot of falconry handling experience available for volunteers or Zookeepers to gain the skills in this area. Sadly, you cannot have a bird of prey as a pet in Australia. Although falconry is not illegal, it is illegal to keep any type of bird of prey in captivity without the appropriate permit, which is not easy to get. Here in Australia, we do not practice falconry with birds of prey. Only a few places offer displays to the public.

When working with birds of prey or raptors, I became familiar with handling chopped up chicks or mice in a leather pouch for training, and this can take some effort to get used to. It's smelly and feels rubbish on your hands. Serious self-hygiene needs to be practiced to avoid salmonella. Whilst having the privilege of working with owls, eagles, etc. in zoos, the visitors are shocked that feeding a bird of prey a clean piece of chicken breast from the supermarket is not sufficient.

A bird of prey needs to eat the fur, feathers and bones to survive. You need to offer a dead chick, mouse or rat on a daily basis and as a Zookeeper you will become comfortable in doing so.

I enjoyed working with these magnificent birds of prey, and learning a very old tradition that dates back to approximately the 13th century was a pleasure. The skills I learnt overseas became valuable for me on my return to Australia in predator training for an endangered mammal species and display work for education at a zoo. I have seen that the few people who are not that keen on animals always cave in and become fascinated when they see a beautiful owl up close on a glove. You will win people over with these birds.

I once worked in a large zoo in WA, on a specialised section that bred endangered animals like the little Dibbler (a small marsupial) for release. I had to spend a few hours a day preparing food for little carnivorous animals. My duties involved me chopping dead pinky mice and rats. I was trained to do this frozen and in a particular way and a certain size. It's certainly not pleasant, but it was a requirement of me as a Research Zookeeper. At this stage of my life, I had been a vegetarian for 15 years, but this never stopped me from preparing the correct food for the animals. There are no excuses. We cannot pick the nice duties, it's all part of the job.

 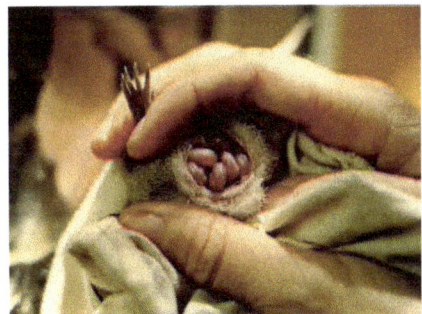

Another test for me when working in a zoo in the UK specialising in big cats was seeing large dead animal bodies ready to be chopped up. I was working closely with the Curator in a zoo that held a large display of big cats. I spent time in and out of the office in the zoo and on this occasion I was looking for Zookeepers out in the grounds and found them doing the job of dealing with a stillborn calf that had been dropped off by a local farmer a few minutes earlier. It was being chopped up to be fed out to the lions and tigers. It was bloody, messy, smelly and really not pretty. This dead animal was a free donation and good food that was being recycled and fed out. It's a sight us Zookeepers need to get comfortable with even though it's not pretty and a little disturbing. I recently heard this saying, *'How do you know if you have a vegan around? They will let you know!'* Yes, that's funny, so maybe best to keep it to yourself, because in the zoo world it's very irritating.

One thing all Zookeepers have in common is that animal deaths can be a difficult one. It doesn't matter how, when or why, it can be horrendous. Animals which die naturally, accidentally or are euthanized for health reasons or for food is sad, but still a big part of doing our duties. No one wants to do this part, but it's a fact of life in the animal world and should be done with no fuss and respect. Certainly, if anyone in the world enjoys euthanizing any animal, maybe you need to look at another career! Even with the best care, the best Zookeepers and best technology, we cannot save everything. Animals do not always make it, whatever is done. This part of the job can definitely be hard on anyone's mental health, and it can really affect the Zookeeper.

Always Enrichment

On a lighter note, a fun part of a Zookeeper's role is to provide enrichment to the animals. The visitors enjoy watching the love and commitment the Zookeeper has to the zoo animal, and can also reassure sceptical visitors. All Zookeepers should know that animal enrichment is not an extra, but important and part of the Zookeeper's daily routine. We always make time to provide this. It's not about making the enclosure look nice with perhaps the wrong but nicer looking fodder or about making the Zookeeper feel accomplished. Its reason is to enrich the animals' day.

Enrichment items are not always food. Stimulation can be created with a smell or an object, sprinklers, some shit from another animal, flowers, nuts, a walk, some attention, a rattling object, etc. As Zookeeper training develops our skills, we will come up with new ideas but, it's not about 'reinventing the wheel'. A lot of ideas have been done over the years, but you never know, so we should always run our ideas by someone that has years of experience to make sure it's safe and OK to try. As a Zookeeper, I enjoyed providing this and then going to the front of the enclosure to watch the animal investigate its new enrichment. It's vital to go to the front of the enclosure to check it from that angle. Seeing what the visitors see is helpful. Enrichment does not just stimulate, but brings out the animals to display better for the paying visitors. All animals deserve this. Mike always provided the elephants with fun activities that they enjoyed. One was the enrichment by painting with their trunks.

The paintings are interesting and can also be sold or used for fundraising. The ideas are endless. Some apes like to use cameras, so old cameras can be intriguing for their smart brains. A simple hose down with a good pressure water hose can be very enriching to animals, like an emu or parrot and the visitors love to see this.

I certainly learned heaps about enrichment when I gained a very young male Gang Gang Cockatoo that was born in a zoo but was not doing well in this environment. Unfortunately, whilst at the zoo, this cockatoo became a feather-plucker due to not receiving enough attention or suitable enrichment. Part of his diet was casuarinas and gumnuts to chew—these birds are real demolition experts! Gang Gang Cockatoos are notorious for not keeping well in captivity, and it is very demanding to meet their needs in a zoo environment.

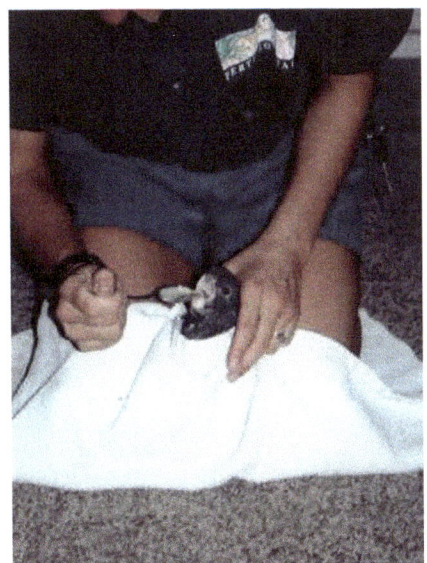
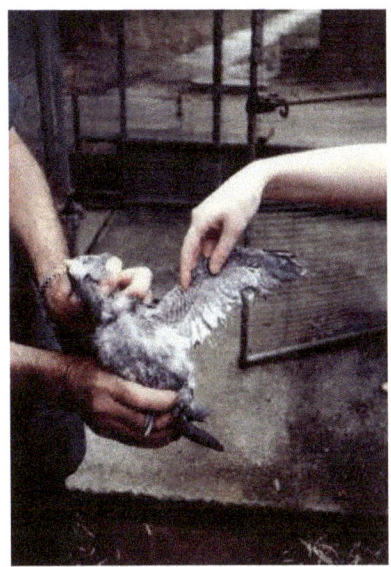

Stages of my Gang Gang Cockatoo's development.

The zoo found a new home for him—that was me. Within a few months of owning this cheeky bird by supplying heaps (and I mean heaps!) of branches of native nuts, he stopped feather plucking. I grew so much from this cheeky bird and continue to use the skills I gained from owning this adorable cockatoo who I formed a close relationship with, to other species of birds in captivity under my care. *Cockatoos will always be one of my favourite animals because of this bird. I love the noisy, cheeky, smart and loving animals they are.*

Always Roar Like a Lion

Remember, if you go along and ignore the standard of work that has been delivered, then that means you are accepting the standard. There are times when you need to speak up and use your voice, you cannot just be a yes person when working as a Zookeeper, sorry to say there will be conflict sometimes. After I had approximately three years' experience, I gained a Zookeeper position as a koala handler in Queensland for a private zoo for a short time. I loved working with the koalas. They were adorable. There were about 20 friendly koalas, all were used for handling, for weddings, busloads of tourists that wanted a photo holding the popular koala. At this Zoo they had an external photographer that provided this service.

Your main job whilst working with koalas is supplying fresh species of eucalyptus leaves; their only food. These animals are a high maintenance, specialized eater. They need to be offered around 6 species of leaves a day. There are 500 species of eucalyptus. Koalas only eat around 50 species of them and only eat the tips. To offer good animal welfare, there is a handling list. This allows the koalas to have rest days to avoid over-handling. You need to keep to the handling list, otherwise certain koalas will be overused, which is definitely not acceptable.

I was employed as an experienced Zookeeper, and on a busy day lots of buses filled with tourists arrived. A couple of the koalas were not co-operating, as they had become tired and, by their behavior, it was obvious they did not want to continue. I informed the photographer that they needed a rest. We are the voice for the animals, but the photographer was not impressed. A non-animal person not trained in this area, then informed me to make the koala sit on the tourist for their photo or take one of the resting koalas off display and use one of those.

This did not sit well with me, and I refused. Unfortunately, the photographer was a friend of the Curator and did not respect my experience or my decision. He suggested I squeeze the koala's wrist and place the koala onto the customer to continue with the photos. I felt this was really not fair on the koalas as they had done many that day and as a qualified, trained, experienced Zookeeper, I felt we had to consider the animals' welfare over the paid photo. On this occasion, I had the confidence to stand up and say no, but I'm not sure many of the new inexperienced Zookeepers would have done the same.

I also had to hold a young female wombat for talks. As you can see from my face, I was not that impressed and, like me, she got cranky and would bite sometimes, which bloody hurt!

As you can imagine, I received some flack for this action. Yes, some people may say you're just being difficult, but that's a cop out. Nothing would change or improve if people throughout history did not stand up. Today, fifteen years later, I heard that one of the most famous koala-holding zoos in Queensland, (not the one I worked at), has finally stopped offering koala holding to the public. Many places in WA are doing the same. The koala is being respected, and at the same time, offering the public a close up encounter for 15 minutes under a controlled manner with no holding. This Zoo confirmed the feedback they have received over the years was to offer something else. This is the new way to appreciate the unique koala and to protect them in captivity.

A few years later, when I went overseas in Europe, miles away from Australia, my skills as a koala keeper certainly helped me gain a position working on a eucalyptus plantation in the UK. You never know where your skills lead to you next. This eucalyptus plantation supplied zoos in Europe with eucalyptus leaves for koalas twice a week. I picked the branches, packed them, keeping the leaves fresh at all times and drove the leaves to the local airport for them to be delivered around Europe all in a few hours for the koalas in zoos.

Home Sweet Home – Animal Enclosures

Here is a good time to mention that to the visitors (and to some management!) the purpose of enclosures is to view an animal, but to Zookeepers, it's the animals' home where they should feel safe and secure. Enclosures in zoos are very important, and Zookeepers will do a lot of cleaning and refurbishing of these spaces.

Both of us are in agreement that once you have gained a good few years of experience and have been trained well, you will start to notice more about enclosures. The minimum size of an enclosure, cage, and aviary for each species is vital. The correct materials, location, where it faces, positioning of feeding bowls, correct feeding areas and shelters all need to be considered. Knowing your species, which ones do well in a mixed exhibit and which mammal and bird can be housed together are all the skills we gained in our training.

Without training, errors affecting the animals will happen. Disappointingly, we recently heard at a small zoo near us that inexperienced and naïve Zookeepers made an impulsive decision that caused an animal welfare issue. We were sad to hear this, and know that an experienced, knowledgeable, skilled Senior Keeper would have never allowed a live ground bird to be put into an aviary that housed a possum overnight. I am sure you can imagine that this bird had nowhere to go and was found by another inexperienced Zookeeper the next day half eaten. This was a bad call that could have been avoided by this inexperienced Zookeeper if a trained, experienced Senior made these important decisions. Learning from your mistakes is not an excuse when working with animals.

You do not have to be a Zookeeper to notice that zoos have evolved significantly over time and there are lots of different enclosure designs now. We know from working in all sizes of zoos that larger zoos have more funding to offer grander enclosures. However, much time and money can be wasted if the Zookeepers are not involved in helping with the design. The Zookeeper is the expert in the animals' needs and their behaviour.

Some enclosures can look good for the visitors but do not consider the function and habitat for the animals which is disappointing for us Zookeepers, and possibly for the general public if they knew this choice. Zookeeper's requirements and our recommendations are valuable, but not always heard. We know this from Mike's experience whilst working with elephants, one of the smartest, popular and long-lived animals kept in captivity. Mike had to raise heaps of his concerns and put forward his recommendation with the new enclosure design for the elephants. Some were taken on, but many were ignored, which is always sad as the Zookeeper has to work with inadequate enclosures that could have been constructed better. Too often an architect under the guidance of the management will design the enclosure without the Zookeeper's input, not knowing the strength of the species. Mike tried on many occasions to gain a bigger pool for the male elephant. It was too small for him, but they offered more room for the visitors with a larger sitting area. Unfortunately, this male elephant was given a small pool, which he sadly lived with for over 15 years. Thankfully, the elephant is finally going to be transferred to an open plain zoo in the near future, which will allow the elephants to explore a vast area. Most elephants are displayed now in an open range zoo with a multi-generational herd.

In the past, zoos primarily displayed animals as curiosities. Enclosures were often stylized and focused on showcasing individual species. Hidden barriers like moats created a more natural looking environment and allowed multiple species to coexist.

In today's modern approach, enclosures emphasise realistic, natural designs. Some zoos create entire ecosystems with real plants, multiple species and immersive walkways for visitors. An impressive enclosure is an aviary. The largest free flight aviary in the world is in South Africa and stands 180ft high on 5 acres, now that is some aviary.

Whilst working as a penguin keeper, seal keeper and a polar bear keeper, I know that enclosures with pools of water and water holes for animals are popular with the visitors. It's great to watch them swim under water; you feel like you are with them. The fact is these enclosures are one of the most expensive to run with a continuous supply of power, a chemical system, heat or cooling systems adding to its high maintenance cost.

Training and Befriending the Animals

Zookeepers will always participate in animal training. A good training program is vital to helping zoos take care of their charges. The animals in zoo collections aren't being trained for obedience the way we train domesticated pets; instead, they're learning how to cooperate with their Zookeepers as part of their daily routine.

This includes how to showcase natural behaviours on cue for educational programs, and even how to participate voluntarily in their own veterinary care. While most people think of 'exotic animal training' as the whips immortalized in old images, modern zoos have chosen voluntary, reward-based training methods that make training sessions some of the most enriching parts of an animal's day. The type of training used almost exclusively in zoos is called 'positive reinforcement training'. Positive reinforcement means that the trainer is adding something to the interaction to make a behaviour more likely to happen again. So when an animal does something that the trainer is looking for, they let the animal know with a marker noise (generally by saying "yes" or "good", or by using a whistle or clicker) and then reward them by giving them something the animal really likes. While this type of training sounds pretty intuitive and like something you might have done with your own domestic pets, it's actually very heavily rooted in the science of how animals learn.

Zookeepers need to be consistent with their training and follow the instructions as trained to do. A large male elephant is trained under protected contact.

Training for most dangerous animals, like bears, primates, lions, etc., is performed behind a fence or barrier for safety. Targets and cues are used for the safety of the keeper whilst performing daily husbandry tasks, such as trimming tusks, hoof work, or daily baths. One of the elephants' favourite foods was sweet potato, and on certain occasions, Mike would use honey sandwiches and even gummy bears (lollies) to feed their sweet tooth. The trick is to find something that motivates the animal to cooperate. Please note that food was never withheld. These skills can be transferred to all animals.

Mike also worked at a camel farm in his own time. He gained a lot of skills handling camels from a very experienced Cameleer. The Cameleer was so passionate about his camels and the experience he was offering, but he wanted and needed to retire, and so he really pushed for Mike to take the business on.

He could see Mike had the passion, confidence and experience for all his loved camels. The successful business offered popular camel walks along the Bibbulmun track and also sold camel milk. We considered this, but the farm was in a very public area of joint ownership with other facilities, which we both felt may be an issue down the track for us.

Animal Handlers and Zookeepers may end up participating in funny animal events. These events can be demanding and stressful, but it can also be fun and rewarding. Mike had to perform an unusual event with the camels. The owner and Mike drove two adult camels into the city, parked up and unloaded these camels right in the heart of the shopping area for a charity event 'Camel Humps for Purple Bra Day'. For a few hours, the general public could meet and greet the camels with a large purple bra on their hump, and this created a good awareness for the campaign. At all times, the camel and the public's safety were considered. It can be stressful for the Cameleers (Zookeepers), but the event gained good awareness for a great cause.

One of the perks of the job is hand-raising animals. It is certainly a dream, but it's no 'bed of roses'. It is mentally and physically draining to perform. There will be problems and even deaths from it which can be soul destroying, but it's definitely something to consider for a dedicated Zookeeper. Zookeepers need to follow instructions from the Senior Zookeeper, Head Keeper, Curator and vet department, as all zoos are under breeding protocols. All Zookeepers will be guided and have strict procedures to follow under a mentor and depending on the situation, a lot of the animals may not be encouraged to tame up. This means avoiding the animal being imprinted—recognising the Zookeeper as parents.

Good zoos do not let the animals just breed with whatever mate when the zoo wants a new baby animal to attract the public in. Zoos hold studbooks for their animals. These are run by Zookeepers (Studbook Keeper) that have been in the zoo world for a while. Studbooks hold all the information on that particular species around the world. The Zookeeper is guided by this. Some private zoos may have more flexibility than other zoos. Breeding animals for the sake of it and having surplus animals is not the aim, so care is taken. Unfortunately, accidents happen. Birthing of animals may come with some problems, and the Zookeeper will need to step in. This is avoided as much as we can as hand-raising comes with other problems and being raised by the mother or father is always the best. If it does arise, then it's an amazing opportunity—hard work with hand-raising—but a huge learning and a memorable moment. We have personally raised many animals for zoos from flamingos, penguins, cockatoos, to snakes, heaps of different marsupials, some endangered or critically endangered animals, some native water rats and a camel were hand-raised under our care.

I have found out that when hand raising animals in my own time and not for zoos, it can also be very costly financially, but very gratifying and much more. I am very much aware that these animals are not my animals just because I have put all the hard work in with hand-raising these precious living things. It's not easy, but *extreme care is always needed when hand-raising wildlife to be returned to the wild to avoid taming. It's vital for their survival in the wild that we get it right.*

Around the world, there are different laws for keeping animals for educational purpose, raising wildlife for release and strict rules for keeping wildlife as pets. Different countries have their own problems with wildlife coming into contact with the public. It's interesting to know and when you visit these countries, it's always best to do your research. The public love to feed wildlife, like ponies, squirrels and bears, but all can cause serious issues for everyone. Here in Australia, we have had issues with dingoes coming into contact with humans and food. The public feeding dingoes in the wild then running to the media when the dingo may bite or be a nuisance is disturbing. Yes, wildlife can behave incorrectly, but people need to be accountable for their own actions and be sensible about mixing with wildlife.

Unnecessary deaths of the animals have happened by authorities, which could have been avoided with more education. Any wild animal coming into contact with the human race feeding them will encourage issues. It's so tempting to do, but avoiding this can certainly help all. For example, in Russia there appear to be many wild bears that are comfortable getting close to humans and taking food from them. This has resulted in many people being killed due to encouraging the animal to come close by offering food.

Hand-raised animals that are tame can also be a problem sometimes. They are not afraid of humans, which often can cause conflict. Here in Australia a few years ago, it came to light that a person who had hand raised a kangaroo and owned it for many years was found dead at his home. It was believed that the tame kangaroo may have attacked the person and gave a fatal kick to the owner. People see these animals as gentle wildlife and most of the time they are, but unfortunately situations can change causing these incidents.

Zookeeper Talks

Wherever I worked as a Zookeeper it was part of my duty to deliver keeper talks, presentations and run interactive animal enclosures on a daily basis. When starting out, this certainly doesn't appeal to most of us and causes a little panic to your day, but it soon disappears once you learn and build up your knowledge and confidence. I was terrified to stand up in front of people at first.

Apparently, Mike felt the same, but you would never know this. He delivers his talks with pure enthusiasm in a fun manner; his fear was obviously very temporary. Once you know what you are talking about, it does become easier to present, but some Zookeepers present more naturally than others.

Keeper talks need to be delivered with personality, positivity and passion, and once you are confident, it's easy to achieve with joy. We have found that it helps to add humour and create your own style. I have learnt that too many facts will bore the audience and so your message will not sink in.

Facts must be correct, or the Zookeeper will lose credibility. When doing talks, you soon realise that delivering presentations is mentally tiring so all Zookeepers need to take turns.

Zoo studies on visitor viewing signs have shown that signs on enclosures are looked at for a few seconds before the visitors move on. In the same way, they will not stay if a keeper talk lacks enthusiasm or interest.

It's vital to connect and engage the visitors when delivering a keeper talk and adjust the delivery to match the audience. The Zookeepers must watch the animals at all times whilst interacting with the public so it can be demanding. We have seen many keeper talks, and some have been frankly embarrassing to watch and cringy to listen to. It's a Zookeeper's duty to deliver information in a good manner with confidence and accuracy. Both Mike and I enjoy delivering keepers talks, from hating them at the very start.

I remember one of my first big keeper talks here in WA at the new penguin exhibit 'open day'. I had to face the audience with a microphone. It was scary! The area was packed with people, and what made it an even more memorable event was the 'mateship' of about 10 Zookeepers in my section who came along to support me… or was it to take the piss and have a giggle? Well, whatever! I enjoyed being part of the Zookeeper team.

Whilst working in a new zoo in the UK, I had to give a seal presentation. One morning, I was performing target training to a very large crowd with a microphone on. I was the Senior Zookeeper and my colleague, another Zookeeper, was presenting with me. The local press were present and as I was performing this presentation, the male seal burped in my face—a very loud burp! The whole crowd heard it. The smell was terrible, but it was funny, and I joked about it and incorporated it into my presentation. I am sure kids will remember their visit that day.

Another popular animal which I enjoyed working with was the penguin. Each day, approximately 50 African Penguins performed a penguin march. This consisted of me entering the enclosure with a metal bucket, putting on their march music, and then they followed me in a line down to the pool. I would have a mic on, and the crowds would laugh and enjoy the funny waddle that penguins do. With my assertive voice, I would welcome everyone but then ask the audience to keep quiet so they would benefit more whilst I presented a talk with the penguins around me. I enjoyed presenting this educational talk, and the happiness the penguins brought to the visitors was important. Even though no one had any idea that I smelt fishy all day from working with these quirky animals.

Now, one of my favourite creatures is the little hedgehog, so it was a joy to work with them, even though they're not the easiest animal to handle. When I was a Hedgehog Keeper in the UK, presenting four talks a day, it was important to educate and inspire the audience for those 15 minutes. Whilst growing up in the UK, there were plenty of hedgehogs around, but today they are hardly seen and the general public at these talks hadn't realised the decline. I explained that these mammals were once common across Europe, but urban development has pushed them out. I managed to get across to around 200 people at each talk the awareness that these cute and popular hedgehogs are near-threatened on the red list after a 30%

decline over the past decade. It was enjoyable to offer this information to hopefully help people support ongoing conservation to save them. This is what it's all about and satisfying.

In 2025, it was pleasing to see some great work has continued in the UK. Mike and I were fortunate enough to join some fellow wildlife carers at the below centre, all run by volunteers with dedication and professionalism. 'Hogwatch Dumbarton Hedgehog Rescue' in Scotland is a rescue, rehabilitation and teaching centre, specialising in critical care for hedgehogs. They have been actively involved in hedgehog conservation efforts, providing life-saving care and promoting education and community engagement. *A good job done.*

Whilst working with these species, I found out that hedgehog's decline was also due to the badger being protected. Badgers are hedgehogs' number one predators. This has caused the tip in the ecosystem, which certainly needed to be adjusted. I could see that protecting one species has sadly sacrificed another species, which is not good enough. Let's hope that the conservationists and scientists act soon to turn this around.

Another time, here in Australia, I was participating in a bird presentation. Whilst holding a majestic wedge-tailed eagle on my arm, the bird of prey opened his wings out. The corner of his large wing caught my eye, which then streamed with tears, but we all carried on and explained (demonstrated!) how amazing the wingspan was.

Difficult Zookeeper talks are the ones interrupted by outside influences. Whilst working in a mixed exhibit talking to the visitors, a jabiru (a large stalk) jabbed a duckling swimming by. It tossed the little duckling in the air and swallowed it in one. This was not easy for sensitive people watching on. Then a wild native common brushtail possum that lived within the zoo grounds entered an enclosure and the visitors had to witness a possum being played with, then thrown out of the enclosure off the top platform through the sky and torn to pieces in the orangutan outdoor exhibit. Another difficult situation for everyone to view.

It's common for wild animals to accidentally enter enclosures. It can be looked upon as enrichment for the captive animals even though it's an uncomfortable sight for many people and for the Zookeeper to explain, but some things are just out of the Zookeeper's control. Then, of course, you have people talking, kids crying and playing, so it can be full on when presenting.

Mike and I have noticed that tourists or new people settling here are fearful of some of the animals in Australia, so it's important as Australian Zookeepers that we educate where we can. In their native home, similar animals may not be deadly or maybe they are, and here they're not. It's our duty to help people understand this and give them tools and information to prevent coming into contact with and avoid potentially bad situations, like people killing these animals. We have noticed that many people from Africa are scared of snakes, scorpions, spiders, etc. because in their country there are many venomous varieties that come close to humans. Keeper talks can help in many ways, so delivering this is so important for Zookeepers to do this well.

We are not sure if people ever noticed the importance of Zookeepers before the famous Zookeeper got the message out there for us all. The 'Crocodile Hunter', Steve Irwin, showed all Zookeepers how to do it. We know that the best Zookeepers we have seen are wildly enthusiastic and show deep passion. Mike is naturally like that. It's great to witness, even if they can be intense and eager. It's fun and exciting with animated presentations, and because of this they draw people in. Their passion captures an audience, and they easily make a connection with them. Like Steve Irwin, Mike's passion is obvious, making the listener want to be part of the experience he is offering. All Zookeepers should 'look and learn' from these mentors and develop their own way to offer this experience.

Zookeepers are put in funny situations, and so cannot worry about ego. Some less charismatic Zookeepers need to gain a sense of humour when working with animals. For example, being pissed on is normal and can only be laughed off. We need to show that we are responsible for delivering high standards of animal care, supporting breeding programs, and conducting animal training, but presenting educational talks in a fun, upbeat manner and talking to the visitors in a friendly way whilst working around the zoo is crucial.

Animals Behaving Like Animals

Talking about media coverage, as Zookeepers this following phrase does not sit well with us, and too often is used to describe a terrible crime from a human. Stop insulting animals with *'They behaved like animals'. (Bestial is also often used to describe behaviour that is primitive or uncivilized).* We find this quote used to describe this situation offensive to animals and misquoted. Animals mostly respect and understand the vital co-existence of other species. Generally, animals care about their own food, shelter, reproduction, and love and respect, just like us humans. Animals are loyal, do not judge and offer unconditional love, but sadly do not receive the same from all humans. On the whole, animals will not harm others unless they feel threatened. Parents of animals will nurse babies and can adopt and nurse different species. They love and can treat each other equally, and us humans could learn from this amazing attitude.

The Animal Kingdom is sensitive to social power as well, but the main differences are the proportions and how it is embedded in the 'circle of life'. Humans always want to be the top predator and if they are not, they will attack an animal threatening it, instead of embracing the power of such impressive animals.

Sharks are one of the top predators and only kill and eat others because they are carnivores and need meat to survive. Sometimes humans get in the way, but they do not kill based on an ideology or religion. In the mating season, some animals will become more aggressive for dominance and the right to mate. It is their instinct to reproduce a strong posterity, but they don't just fight for nothing and behave badly like some humans on a Saturday night under the influence of drink, drugs, or misguided egos, pride or plain stupidity. Watching animals helps you to admire the beautiful and genial harmony they show. Unfortunately, humans are still finding it hard to live amicably with all species on this planet. Let's 'look and learn' and do better!

Many Zookeepers who work with primates will see how amazing these species of animals are and how close they are in many ways to us. For me, when I gained an opportunity to work with these stunning primates, *I knew this was not the area for me to work* in; *they are way too much like humans for me.* These animals hold many traits of human intelligence, such as empathy, theory of mind, mourning, ritual, and the use of symbols and tools. These traits are somewhat apparent in great apes (including humans), although they are in much less sophisticated forms than in humans, for example, the great ape language, which is basic. The great apes show some cognitive and empathic abilities. Chimpanzees make tools and use them to acquire foods and for social displays. They have mildly complex hunting strategies requiring cooperation, influence and rank. They are status conscious and manipulative and can learn to use symbols and understand aspects of human language, including numbers.

One common characteristic present in species of "high degree intelligence", like elephants, dolphins and great apes, *including humans,* is a brain of enlarged size. Along with this, there is a more developed neocortex. They are linked to social intelligence and the ability to gauge what another is thinking or feeling. This is also present in bottlenose dolphins, which are popular creatures amongst the general public. As you can see, humans are supposed to be more intelligent than some animals, but sometimes humans behave in an uncivilised and primitive way. How disappointing for us all to witness this terrible behaviour. *Let's hope that us humans evolve better than we have so far as we continue to share this incredible planet.*

Since living in Australia for the last 25 years, I have found out that wildlife can certainly be dangerous to our pets or to ourselves whilst out and about. Before living in Australia, I was really not aware of all this. Roos, emus, snakes and baits can be deadly here, and I have certainly learnt that kangaroos are amazing but can also cause serious car accidents. I avoid driving at dawn and dusk in particular, but care is taken at all times to avoid collisions. I have had many kangaroos jump out in front of me and it's not always possible to avoid hitting them. Yuk! I have certainly had the misfortune of dealing with the sad mess when they both collide.

It's upsetting and just horrible and often you are on your own down a dirt road to deal with it yourself. Not everyone is aware, but it is law to stop and check they are OK, if not to call the ranger or a local wildlife carer to help. Being a registered Wildlife Carer, I have taken in many orphaned joeys that have been rescued or dropped off to a Wildlife Rehabilitation Centre needing to be cared for.

Another one that was not known to me, and probably to city dwellers, was that kangaroos and emus can also be dangerous to your pet dogs. Roos can protect themselves from dogs by delivering an amazing kick with sharp claws, leaving a dog injured or dead, so care needs to be taken walking in the bush. As responsible dog owners, you need to train your dogs to not chase kangaroos. Kangaroos can even get your dog in a headlock and drown the dog holding it under water.

Another danger I was not aware of until I settled in rural Australia was the snakes. All year around, but in particular in the lovely springtime, September/October onwards, snakes become more active, and we need to be aware that they are passing through our property. It should be a nice time of year, but not for me living in the country with pets because venomous snakes can be a problem when you have a dog or cat. We believe snake avoidance training is so important for your dogs and we recommend it for the 'love of dogs'. We participated in a workshop years ago and now offer this quick avoidance training to our own dogs and to friends and family to help save precious dogs to understand and avoid the snake at all times, instead of investigating the snake and getting bitten. We have helped all breeds of dogs with snake alert training, from a tiny Chihuahua to a Great Dane. If the dog plays with a snake and receives a snake bite, it can be deadly and very costly, even if you do get your dog or cat to the vet in time to save it. Unfortunately, we have had friends and neighbours who have rushed their dog to the vet; some dogs make it, and some do not, which is extremely sad.

Growing up on the other side of the world, I was certainly not aware of these everyday issues in other countries. In the UK, you may come across the odd, very mild venomous snake, the adder, or a badger that potentially can be a problem to your dog if you take it for a walk at night, but that's about it.

The next situation we find difficult to support is an important one to be aware of. When walking your dogs in Australia, be aware of 1080 baits (in a shape of sausage) on government land managed by the local DBCA. When considering a nice Sunday walk with your dogs, planning and checking safe places is needed. You cannot take your dogs for a walk anywhere here, like you can in Europe. 1080 is a bait with a poisonous plant ingredient added to it, which can be very dangerous if your dog consumes it.

The principal is that it does not kill native animals, which is great, but if a domestic dog or cat eats the bait, it's a slow and painful death for these animals and vets will not be able to save the animal showing symptoms. We have heard of many cases of this happening (dogs eating baits outside the restricted drop area).

We're not sure how some of the baits end up in private areas. As Zookeepers, conservationists, landowners, animal lovers, we are not convinced that using these 1080 baits is the answer to control a big problem, like foxes and feral cats. It really does not just target this problem, given the high risk of pets/working dogs accidentally dying from eating the 1080 baits, to us this system is not good enough to really support it, well, for us.

Just Another Animal At The Zoo

There's no time to be shy being a Zookeeper. Zookeepers often become the exhibit to watch. The visitors love to watch the Zookeeper at work, it's part and parcel of the role. Some animal sections have bigger cleans than others, but all Zookeepers perform heaps of cleaning. Zookeepers try to get it done before the zoo opens, but sometimes it is not possible.

The visitors especially love to watch the animals playing with Zookeepers whilst cleaning an exhibit or refurbishing it. It's amusing and entertaining to watch naughty parrots, cockatoos, or clever Kea birds from New Zealand stealing your equipment, whilst placing enrichment. A speaking cockatoo laughing whilst performing these naughty acts just adds to the whole experience. We are on display at all times, so Zookeepers should not use mobile phones whilst working in enclosures. Sorry to say, I have seen many other Zookeepers on their phones around the zoo, even in enclosures. Please use your two-way. Not only is it a safety risk, but it also looks so unprofessional.

So often the visitors watch us Zookeepers at work, and then make a joke about the Zookeeper, saying comments like, *'what kind of bird is this one?!'* when working in an aviary, for example. The best thing to do is laugh it off. Watching the Zookeeper get bitten, flown at or chased is funny to the visitors. We have both been bitten by a variety of animals, from a snake, possum, parrot, and even a camel whilst cleaning an exhibit with watchful eyes on us. But these days we can be captured on the mobile phone and put out on social media, making us famous without knowing it. The public will take photos of you, so you need to just get on with it. We have to try to juggle our daily routines with lots of eyes watching on and can't be embarrassed. We have to enjoy the experience and 'Carry on'! recognising it is another work hazard for Zookeepers.

TRAVELLING ZOOKEEPERS

Being a qualified trained Zookeepers means you can work anywhere in the world. There are only four zoos in WA and a few other places to gain animal work, so jobs are limited. However, there is an opportunity to go interstate or overseas to gain a position, which is a cool thing to do.

Whilst Mike was gaining specialized training in the elephant world and working his way up to the Head Elephant Handler from the Senior Zookeeper position, I took a different direction, gaining experience overseas. I decided I want to explore the Zookeeper world in different zoos and meet other people to advance my skills. I applied for a position to attend a highly regarded 3-week conservation course in the Channel Islands. It's competitive to gain a spot, but I did, and the zoo paid for the course.

I decided to extend the trip and participate in a 3-month keeper exchange. I found someone at a zoo in the UK that wanted to work as me here in Australia and I filled their position in the UK for 3 months. On this course you meet some interesting people around the world in the animal and conservation field. I made some amazing new friends from other countries, which I still stay in contact with.

One of my contacts lives in New York. Ten years later, I managed to visit the USA and met up with her and saw first-hand the great work she achieved in her country. Firstly, when the twin towers were attacked in the USA, she was one of the main people who organised all the pets locked away in apartments, waiting for their owners to come home. She collected many animals, from parrots to cats and dogs. It was just amazing to hear how she stepped in and made a difference to all the loved pets left behind in this tragedy.

My friend was not a Zookeeper but worked in Primate Rescue Centres or zoos in the USA, offering mental support to ex-pet primates, like chimpanzees. All her work was fund-raised charity work, and I was fortunate to attend one of the upmarket art gallery events in New York, which displayed some beautiful black and white photography of chimpanzee images.

Whilst out in her world, wining and dining in New York City, I met one of her close friends, which is one of the richest ladies in the USA. The main item we had in common was that she was an animal lover and donated money to a lot of different animal charities. It was a pleasurable afternoon tea with this lady, sitting discussing the great work that all types of people are participating in for the good of the Animal Kingdom.

From travelling and working in different zoos, I became more confident in my field and got involved in publishing articles in specialised magazines on my return to Oz. Over the years, I have managed to get three articles in the highly regarded BirdKeeper Magazine.

Then I was given the opportunity to successfully breed some Rainbow Beeeaters in captivity, and my subsequent husbandry article was published in ARAZPA Magazine. I bred Rainbow Beeeater for the first time at this zoo in WA under the supervision of my Curator. It was known in the bird world that it was difficult breeding these birds in captivity. I was dedicated, followed instructions, and it took a lot of time and patience, extra live food and the correct substrate for them to be comfortable to dig out a tunnel and nest in. With this experience, I shared my knowledge with a Zookeeper overseas that was also trying to breed Bee-eaters at their amazing bird park in Singapore.

On my first stop out of Australia, I managed to gain some valuable experience working in a zoo and an amazing Bird Park in Singapore, Asia. I have not worked with many megafauna, so when I got the opportunity to work with the Zookeeper who looked after the new polar bear exhibit in Singapore, it was a hard 'yes'. The pure awe of this creature, the size, the strength, the intelligence, certainly made me feel very small. Humans are pretty irrelevant next to these magnificent animals. Laying out its food in its night quarters and waiting to open up the slide was exciting. I was under strict health and safety rules whilst working with the other Zookeeper. I was informed to stay away from the edge of the slide (metal divider between the night quarters and the enclosure on display) as the polar bear would hit the slide with its massive hand/arm to force it open quicker, and if you stood in the way, you could get hit by the slide. I loved watching this awesome bear come into his area to enjoy his good variety of food. The size of its head and paws was gobsmacking.

Another one of these experiences at the same zoo was being off display with the alpha male chimpanzee—a huge powerful creature spending time in his night quarters. This chimp was very vocal—screaming, climbing, jumping, hanging off his bars, showing his teeth. He was frustrated because he wanted to get out to join his troop on display and was highly impatient with the wait. Wow, I thought, humans have no chance, and I felt my insignificance in being a lesser species. This definitely should be experienced by human beings some time in their life, to put us top predators in our places.

Whilst working in Singapore, I stayed at the 'Keepers Lodge', which was down a long driveway near the zoo. Being Asia, it was very humid with a tropical landscape. I had been out visiting the Night Zoo, so I was arriving back by taxi around 10.00pm. The taxi driver stopped at the entrance of the drive and wanted me to get out. I said, yes this is it, but further down the road. The taxi driver replied that he would not be driving down this road due to the many large, retic pythons near the jungle.

I thought he was joking, but he wasn't, and he was not going to drive down there. Shit! WTF! I thought. It was dark. I had no torch and there were seriously large pythons lurking in the bushes. Even as a Zookeeper, I was not keen and, frankly, scared. Unfortunately, I had no choice but to do this. My heart was beating so bleeding hard I thought it was going to burst.

I walked right in the middle of the road, hoping I could get to the house without being taken by a massive python. Yes, I survived. The next day, when working with Zookeepers, one of their jobs was to set the traps up off display amongst the enclosures to catch the nuisance wild retic pythons at the zoo. We certainly do not have this problem in Europe or Australia. But all Zookeepers need to deal with all pests (including some of the public) on a day-to-day basis.

Whilst travelling around the world as a member of the public, visiting and working at different zoos, I found it can be difficult not to be critical. As soon as we enter the place, we will get a vibe or opinion of the zoo. It's natural to look at every enclosure and see what is wrong, what needs to be done, or what is good. We know that non-Zookeepers just do not see what we see.

As Zookeepers we smell things that the general public will not smell and see things that may look OK to the visitor or to a non-trained eye, but deep down we know it's not good enough. It's obvious to an experienced Zookeeper what needs to be done to improve this. We can spot mice and rat holes and can smell when they're present.

I have said to many people, visiting Zookeepers are like chefs eating out at a restaurant or café. We are passionate about what we do. Chefs will know what is wrong with the dish, the ambiance of the place and what it is lacking. All Zookeepers need to keep in the back of their mind that someone (from another zoo) might be visiting your zoo and work hard to get it right. We are proud or should be proud of what we have achieved, and not knowing who will be watching certainly keeps you on your toes. Just like the famous chef Gordon Ramsey critiquing a restaurant!

Later on in my career, I received a classic (stupid) comment from a 'non-animal manager' working in a small zoo and not understanding a Zookeeper's position. They asked me when I returned to work after visiting four zoos whilst on holiday. *'Why would you do that? You need to rest up and do some fun things.'* Seriously, how ridiculous! This is fun for a Zookeeper; like a person who enjoys visiting restaurants, eating and drinking wine! It's our passion and feeds a Zookeeper's soul, but it's certainly not worth trying to explain to people not on the same wavelength, the interest of animals.

I would like to give some advice to people on holiday because over the years, I have met people who say they are animal lovers, but then they tell me whilst on holiday they experienced a cuddle with a chimpanzee or rode a baby elephant. They have visited dolphins and whale shows, not really understanding the whole implication in doing so. I witnessed this aspect whilst working in a popular Asian zoo. Tagging along with a primate keeper, I experienced what really happens, and it was uncomfortable to deal with.

This particular zoo offered a photo with baby chimpanzees, which was popular with the visitors. I worked with the Zookeepers who were responsible for caring for the animals used in these events. Chimpanzee babies are adorable to everyone, and it was a demanding event. Little did I know the impact of these human needs on the animals involved.

We collected the baby chimp and cycled up to the event area for a short time for photos. The public loved this event, and the chimp appeared to be OK with it. However, returning the baby chimp back to the group is where the unpleasant reality happened. Chimpanzee babies are just adorable, but once they start to grow up, they need to be reintroduced back into the troop. That's when you see what us humans are doing.

This baby chimpanzee was subject to aggression from other chimps. He had to be accepted back into the troop, so it started with an introduction in size and status, up to the alpha male. The alpha male chimp in the night quarters next door was pretty intimidating whilst this was happening. He was hanging off the bars, screaming with excitement and anger. This baby chimp screamed in the night quarters.

I just had to ignore it, carry on chopping up fruit and veg and only intervene with a water hose if it got out of control. Eventually, this baby chimp is accepted back in and can live with the troop full time. This was very frightening to be part of. It was so aching to witness. I wouldn't have wanted to do this on a regular basis, but hats off for the Zookeepers that needed to perform this and the care they showed was good.

The Zookeepers did everything they could for these animals—they loved them—but it was management/owners that required them to perform. This really is a problem we have created for our own needs, and I am sure if people had experienced what I had, they would say we could live without this experience. This practice is what zoo haters would definitely be against. Luckily, things are evolving all the time in this area. We know as we have recently visited this zoo and these experiences no longer exist, so now Zookeepers do not need to participate in this difficult duty.

Different countries have different attitudes and policies that are acceptable for their culture, which can be challenging at times. Whilst mixing with other Zookeepers around the world, I have found out that certain actions can be OK in their country. One was feeding out young dead lions (not cub stage) that had no gene purpose to other animals in the zoo collection, which is acceptable in Denmark. Where other Zookeepers in other countries would not be permitted to do this action as it would not be ethical. Australia certainly has stricter rules than some other countries.

It's not uncommon for passionate Zookeepers to use annual leave to attend courses to improve their knowledge. We have often both done this and never regret it. When Mike was working on the Nocturnal House, he expressed an interest to his Curator in attending a specialised course for Tasmanian Devils that was being run by a wildlife park in Tasmania. This course became a new requirement to participate in if you were working with these species in a zoo. The main reason was the outbreak of a devil facial tumour that was taking over the wild Tassie devils. Attending this course was very beneficial to his position and to the zoo.

Similarly, whilst I was overseas attending the 3-month keeper exchange in the UK, I was made aware of a conservation program that this zoo was participating in with wild penguins in South Africa. A few years later, I applied and organised a 3-week experience, helping with oiled, injured, orphaned and rehabilitated penguins and attended a release. The skills I learnt from these great people, the experience and contacts I made were very fulfilling. One of the skills which is becoming vital to most countries is dealing with disasters like oil spillage affecting seabirds and how to treat them in these emergencies. These skills are transferable to anywhere in the world.

The Southern African Foundation for the Conservation of Coastal Birds (SANCCOB) is a ripper of a place, and an excellent set up. It's a charity whose primary objective is to reverse the decline of the seabird population through rescue and rehabilitation. It's a real hands-on experience. Due to my previous experience with working with penguins in zoos, they gave me the responsibility of driving 20 penguins to the harbour to meet a tourist ferry to join them with the boxes of penguins ready to be released. The whole ferry got involved in the release, and it was wonderful to be part of it. But, oh shit! My return was not so amazing. I got lost driving the ute back to the centre and ended up in a suburb that was not so inviting, but I finally made it back in one piece to let everyone know it went swimmingly.

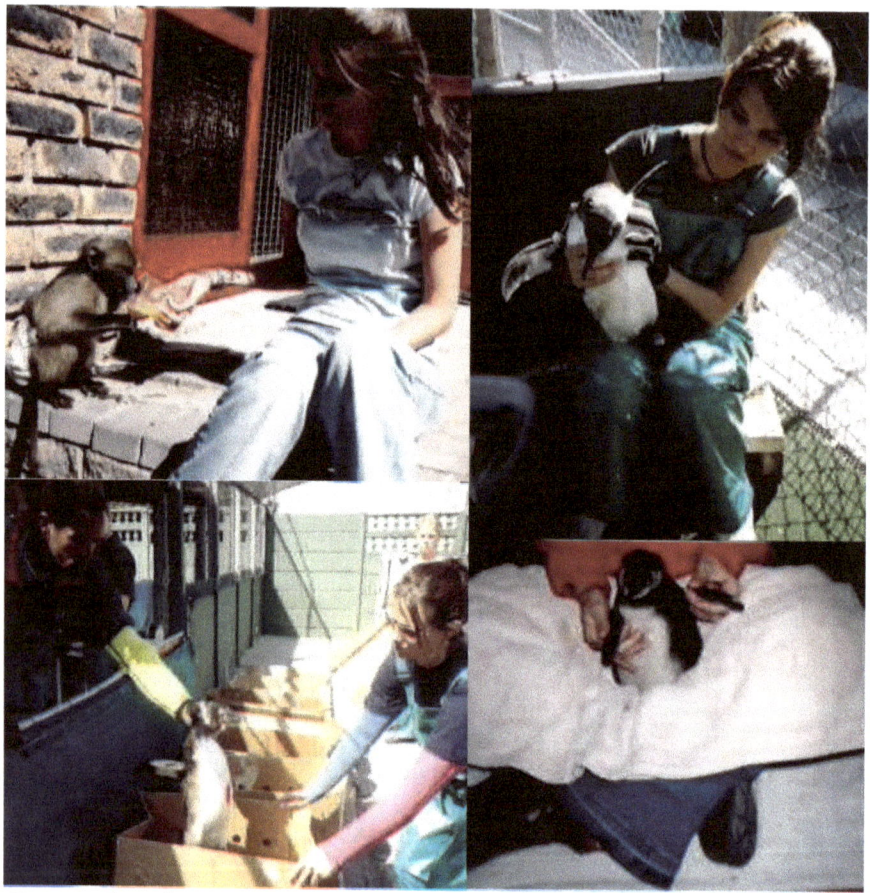

Gaining hands-on experience in the field with the locals (here in Africa) was an amazing opportunity and the ultimate reward for us Zookeepers.

IT'S AN AMAZING JOB

It's amazing how much you gain from this. I attended a turtle count training experience on a Greek island for 2 weeks. It was the hatching season for the local endangered turtles. Every year, people can get involved, watching the little turtles hatch out and run to the ocean. Monitoring these adorable creatures, collecting information for the ongoing research program is vital and another great and empowering experience to be involved in. Then when I returned to Western Australia, I participated with turtle monitoring by attending a 3-week experience on Barrow Island. You work through the night, watching the turtles arrive, slowly climb up the beach and nest. You measure, check and record everything whilst she lays the eggs—but carefully, so you don't disturb her. This was amazing, and I highly recommend having a go. You do not have to be a Zookeeper to gain a position. There are plenty of these opportunities around the world to jump into and get out there and learn. High-profile zoos have relationships with other organisations around the world to suit all interests. There are heaps out there.

It's obvious when you start working in the zoo world that it's a small world. When I met a shearer from WA whilst working at the run-down zoo that was part of the TV series, I did not think I would meet him again in Oz years later, but I did. The only llama at this zoo that needed a long overdue shear was being done by a WA shearer. As a fellow Aussie, I was told to go over and say hi to this shearer. What a great job he did! This llama was pretty feral. Ten years later, I met the same shearer here in WA who sheared Mike's alpacas in Perth and lives in the southwest like us. He is still our shearer. What a chuckle to meet him again. *What a crazy small world it is!*

Wildly Famous – Meet the Celebrities

As well as being in newspapers, on radio stations and on TV ourselves, we have both met a few celebrities over the years. It can be exciting as a Zookeeper meeting famous people whilst out in the zoo or giving a Keeper talk to them. We have had the opportunity to meet famous AFL and soccer players, rugby players, actors and actresses, even prime ministers, so it's important to represent the zoo well and offer a memorable interaction.

Dean Cox, AFL West Coast Eagles player

John Worsfold, a former Australian rules football coach, captain and player

Ian Parmenter, local author and TV presenter

Once, whilst working in a zoo in the UK, I heard that David Attenborough was in a bookshop in the City of Bristol for a few hours. I managed to leave the zoo during my lunch break, rush to the shop, and queue up. The public saw I was in my Zookeeper uniform and let me move closer to the front.

When I got to the signing table, I had my Attenborough book open at the page where I wanted his signature. He asked me why I wanted him to sign on this particular page. I explained that I was presently on a Zookeeper exchange but worked with the animals on that page in Australia. He commented saying that numbats were one of his favourite Australian animals and smiled as he gave me his signature. Well, that was worth it, I thought, trying to fit it into my day, rushing around to meet this highly regarded, well-known presenter of animal documentaries. Later, of course, other Zookeepers who did not make time to achieve this expressed how pissed and jealous they were of my close encounter with David!

It's a Smelly Job

What I can say is when we started out as a Zookeeper, we really did not know the real stuff we would be doing. I had to come to terms quickly that it's definitely not a glamorous job, even though all the reality shows, media coverage, articles and books try to show that it is. Dealing with animal issues on a daily basis might come naturally to Zookeepers but may disgust people out of the zoo world. Most days, us Zookeepers are covered in slobber. My boots will always have shit on them. Hands and arms will be put in some weird places! Hay, feathers, peanuts, even some poo in their hair and snacks in pockets. Drawing blood is one of the skills required, as well as examining shit on a daily basis. Nose and reflux will be tested! There will be odours on clothes. On top of this, you will get bitten, scratched and trodden on (by humans as well as the animals!). There will be unusual cleaning, including teeth, rectal and penis cleaning. It is not unusual to be looking for sperm plugs on your knees in 30 degrees to confirm a successful mating of an endangered animal. Yet all these challenges are some of the best parts of being a Zookeeper. We are more than happy to deal with them any day, but it is the human bullshit of politics, due to insecurity, jealousy or being a bad communicator that is the real squeamish matter we all could live without, and boy, have we met some real challenging characters in this world.

Another wake up call for me was that Zookeepers smell like shit. This came to light, especially when I worked with seals and penguins, chopping up fish all day. The smell gathered on my uniform, body and hair. I got used to the smell and only noticed it was strong when I left the zoo and came out in the real world. I noticed people keeping their distance when I stopped at a fuel station or ran into a shop on my way home. When I finally got home, I was made to strip my clothes at the door, as the smell was way too much for anyone else at home.

I was not alone. Mike, on the other side of the world, was experiencing the same reaction with his wife and kids, wanting him to shower and change as soon as he got home. The smell of elephant urine was overpowering to people that had not been working with them all day. Mike did not realise how smelly his clothes were until he had a shower and then picked them up for the laundry basket. *Yes, Zookeepers smell!*

As a Zookeeper, shit is a big part of your day. I certainly surprised myself when working with animals. I was very capable of dealing with smelly shit when it came to animals. One incident was when I was working in a vet practice in the UK, which was more testing than I expected. I had some work as a vet nurse's assistant for a small animal practice dealing mainly with pets like dogs, cats, rabbits, etc, and then for a large animal practice mainly dealing with horses, cattle, pigs, sheep and alpacas. I was surprised how much vets and vet nurses have to deal with humans and their emotions as they drop off their animals and at how much death and counselling a vet nurse or vet nurse assistant has to deal with on a daily basis. It was all very mentally draining.

I give full respect to veterinary staff for providing this valuable service. Keeping calm with emergencies, from a dog attack on a dog, snake bite, to a young builder coming into the practice with his lovely golden retriever with a concerned, tired and embarrassed face. This builder loved his dog, and explained to me at the counter in front of the full waiting room that his dog had gastro and was very poorly. In fact, a lot of dogs over the last few days had gastro, which they had picked up from a nearby park. As he was explaining, his dog produced a fountain of diarrhea. It poured out of the distressed dog, spreading across the vinyl floor with a smell so bad you had to cover your nose and mouth. I quickly took over the situation as the vet nurse assistant. I informed the owner to leave and call us later and addressed the poor dog, who also looked embarrassed. I then had to address the disgusting shit with everyone watching, trying not to retch. What a job! Oh boy, I certainly lost my appetite for lunch that day!

Whilst I cannot watch or be involved in human blood emergencies, operations, vomit, birthing or shit for humans, I can for animals. Some people can cope with this for children, old people, but not for animals. I respect them all for caring for humans, but I know I certainly could not do what they do for humans. However, for animals, I can do and am happy to do so 100%. Luckily, we all have different skills.

On the subject of animal shit, there was another realization that whilst working with animals, looking at shit is normal. A Zookeeper can tell a lot from examining shit. Often you have to collect and test it, and coping with smells on a hot day in a zoo is also something you need to deal with. The fermented smell of dirty bins, maggots hatching, rotten meat and faeces is a normal duty for a Zookeeper. On a Zookeeper's morning tea chat, it came to a vote that the worst smelling shit is from seals and otters, but I am sure these Zookeepers that were not around would say it's not.

Whilst I was working in zoos and veterinary clinics overseas dealing with all kinds of shit, Mike was dealing with some of the biggest poop all day, every day here in Australia. Working with elephants that eat up to 150kg of food a day certainly ends with a lot of poop, so a wheelbarrow and plenty of strength are needed to pick up the piles of poop whilst the visitors watch 4 times a day. Elephants only digest 50% of what they eat so this means 75kg of poop per elephant a day needs to be removed with visitor comments to keep you company! Good Zookeepers will remove this poop not just for presentation but for prevention of flies and to stop any elephants deciding to have a munch on undigested food matter. No one wants to see that! *Now that's a pile of shit! No competition—Mike won on this poo story!*

It's a Dangerous Job

I learnt right from the start that 'Crickey, being a Zookeeper is a dangerous job'! We will be exposed to dangerous situations on a daily basis. From climbing ladders to using power tools, heavy wheelbarrows, equipment and machinery. This means wearing the appropriate clothing like eye protectors, etc. and full concentration with all the animals, their enclosures, including training dangerous animals, are of high priority.

Some sections are more physical than others, so looking after our backs is very important. As Zookeepers we are taught to organise each other to help with heavy work. It's part of the job to remove piles of poo and some sections use a lot of slides for entry into night quarters. Some difficult jobs can be entering enclosures and safely using the slides to lock animals away. Particular care must be taken as humans will make errors, and this can be fatal for Zookeepers or the animals if we 'fuck up'. Recently, a baby gorilla was accidentally killed at a zoo in Canada when it was struck in the head by a door. This 2-year-old gorilla was roaming from room to room when a Zookeeper activated the wrong hydraulic door to separate her. The accident left the ape with serious head injuries. She needed CPR but did not make it. This tragedy struck everyone so deeply, a full investigation and retraining of the Zookeepers will be done to prevent future incidents ever happening again. These Zookeepers may find it hard to come back from this terrible error.

There will be protocols and standard operating procedures (SOPs) that need to be followed at all times. Never take shortcuts, rush or work on our own when it's a two Zookeeper policy. Zookeepers have been injured horribly or killed not following these procedures. We must make sure all Zookeepers we are working with are practicing this too. I have seen, heard and been in accidents whilst working as a Zookeeper, and it's not pleasant. But even when the best OHS is practiced, accidents will happen—working with animals is unpredictable. On one particular morning, I heard the code call for an emergency on the two-way. I kept radio silence but listened on whilst working. A good experienced qualified Zookeeper had been hurt whilst performing training with the sunbears. Her arm had been crushed through a hatch. The Zookeeper was taken to hospital and sadly her arm took months to rehabilitate, and her career was sent backwards.

At no stage did I think the next emergency code call at this zoo would be me. Bugger! I was at the beginning of my career trying to secure my position at the zoo. We were short staffed out on the grounds. I arrived at 7.00 am to start my day as usual, heading to the bird kitchen to join the team for food prep. The whole bird keeping team was chopping up fruit and veggies for all the animals in our section. This was normal—we chopped fruit, veg and prepared food for about 1 hour before we went off to service our animals.

I was instructed to use the very large and daunting meat mincer machine. The meat mincer machine had been at the zoo for years. It was outdated and a little scary to use. The Senior Zookeeper on that day asked me to use the machine but mentioned that no one else around had used it before. I was a little shocked with this comment as I had seen others on it. I had been trained quickly on this machine months prior, so I just got on with doing this duty. I had to put in cattle hearts to mince up the meat and mix with other ingredients for the birds at the zoo.

I had finished putting all the hearts through the machine and I leant forward to turn the machine off at the mains. Then I ducked down to collect the bowl under the outlet. As I cleared the hanging mince, there was an unusual bang. The machine grabbed my right index finger in… and the rest, well, was very messy. All I remember is turning around to the table where approximately 5 keepers were chopping up fruit. The Senior Zookeeper looked at me whilst I said, "I think I have cut my finger." I put my hand up in the air. Blood squirted from my index finger and they responded by saying, "You've done more than cut your f**king finger." Then I fainted onto the cold, wet, hard ground.

Waking up, I found myself sitting on a chair, arm in the air, and everyone running around like 'headless chooks'. Two-ways were being used, and some Zookeepers were looking into the bucket of minced meat. It was obvious later they were looking for the top of my finger to put on ice. The ambulance arrived quickly, whilst other keepers on different sections that started later were arriving *(Mike remembers this code call)*. All I kept thinking was, "I am going to lose my contract and be out of the system!" Nothing else mattered. I look back now and think how ridiculous! What was I thinking, and why did I not put my health first? I had worked so hard, and it was my position at the zoo that was more important than my finger. That's how competitive this world is, a very scary matter.

Next, I arrived at the emergency department, lying down on the stretcher with my arm up, blood all down my arm, my finger throbbing, and the nurses all thinking my story would be more exciting if an exotic animal had bitten my finger off! My British boyfriend at the time arrived with great concern. Still, all I could think of was my Zookeeper contract.

Yes, this accident meant my contract was given to someone else. I was rehabilitated back into the zoo. The machine was taken away by Worksafe and never used again. I did not want to make a fuss to jeopardise my chance to continue as a Zookeeper so I recovered as quickly as I could, rushing back to work without any further treatment. Looking back, I should have spent more time on fixing my finger, which is still not good, but back then I really did not want to make a big deal, even though it was a massive deal.

As well, as machinery and physical job conditions, working with a particular species, like exotic animals, is more dangerous. Most deaths or serious injuries to Zookeepers have been from elephants and big cats like lions and tigers. Sometimes these fatal deaths get raised in the media, but a lot are kept quiet. It's hard to say how many Zookeepers a year get injured or have died around the world, but reading on the Zoochat blog, there are certainly a lot of these incidents that I, who has an interest, have not heard of and it's shocking to read. It appears that most of these tragic attacks or even deaths have been kept out of the media as it's bad publicity for everyone.

Mike worked with elephants for years, and he was always aware that he was at high risk from attacks or an accident. Elephants are classed as the most dangerous animals to work with in captivity, but to the general public, they are gentle giants. They are smart, and very powerful animals, and often you are working with free contact (i.e. closely with them and without a barrier). You can work with them for years, but there is always the risk that one day they could turn and kill you. They are a megafauna that many people love to see, but caution is necessary at all times. Zookeepers who work with elephants have been killed in the past, even though the Zookeeper had a good relationship with this species and worked well with them for some time. These animals are a high-risk animal to work with and can grab any opportunity to take you on.

Mike shared a funny situation with me that could have potentially been very dangerous. When working with elephants, there is always a two-Zookeepers policy in place. This day both Zookeepers were with the three elephants in an outdoor area with approximately 100 people waiting to attend the popular elephant talk. Mike started his 45-minute elephant talk to the large crowd with a mic on. Talking, training and monitoring large animals is not an easy position to be in, as well as making sure the visitors are receiving a positive, upbeat Zookeeper talk. Mike performed free contact training and rewarded them for their actions through small pieces of food. On this day, it was sugar cane. Whilst delivering his talk,

Mike was explaining the trunk, giving commands, feet husbandry, how they only sleep 3 to 4 hours, etc. Elephants have an amazing sense of smell, and they are very smart and powerful. When Mike completed the keeper talk, he walked up to the audience for question time and was joined by the matriarch elephant. She stood alongside him for about ten minutes, waiting patiently and sucking up to him. She knew he had a piece of sugar cane left in his trouser pocket. Mike called the other elephant up to show the tusks as a question came up from the visitors. The elephant, who had a better example of a tusk, lifted her trunk to show them. Mike rewarded her with the last piece of sugar cane. But the matriarch believed *she* was entitled to the last piece. After another elephant received it, the matriarch told the other elephant off by giving her a head butt, and Mike, who was standing in between the two elephants, was knocked flying onto the rocks, landing upside down in a heap. Their speed and power were amazing. The whole crowd gasped in horror. Mike stood up and brushed himself off, whilst he explained what had happened to the crowd. He knew he had screwed up and was so grateful it was just a big push. The female elephant could have killed the Zookeeper.

Instead, it was a warning to show mutual respect.

This incident gave Mike confidence because, whilst she could have killed him, she chose not to. From that day on, he gave his last treat to her when he was working with her at the end of the day. Mike gained even more respect and confidence for working around elephants. He went on to work with this beautiful elephant for another 6 years, ending up as the Head Elephant Keeper. He always says, *'who is training who in zoos?!'*

Mike also found out that when collecting enrichment for animals in captivity, Zookeepers need to take care. Mike went out during his lunch break to cut a lot of fresh grass for the elephants. After cutting and raking it into hessian bags, he returned to the zoo elephant enclosure and emptied the grasses. It was a scary moment to find a venomous tiger snake had sneaked into the bag. Mike called the Reptile Zookeepers to catch the snake and release it back in the area that it must have resided in. Luckily, the elephants did not get to see the snake, as there would have been a lot of noise and drama if they had!

When I started out, I noticed Zookeepers catching Zoonotic diseases which I was not aware of prior. These are infectious diseases transferred from an animal to a human and may be bacterial, viral or parasitic. When working with animals, you will get bitten, scratched and both of us have been accidentally and deliberately bitten by many animals over the years. It is another occupational hazard and no big thing. Whilst precaution was always taken, it still happens, and an incident report is required even for minor bites. Animals will bite and we have experienced nips from a snake, a tarantula, an elephant, cockatoos, penguins, a lizard, a ferret, a camel, possums and a cheeky kangaroo. A large scorpion even managed to sting me. It's really not that bad, and I find it reassuring to know what it feels like, so there is no fear of it happening.

Shit happens when you are working with animals. I remember one time, when I was one of the main experienced bird handlers assigned to catch around 30 Black Cockatoos (gentle birds, but with a big powerful beak) in a large aviary. The birds needed their yearly worming and to be checked together by the vets at the zoo. On this occasion everything went well, but the last bird got me big time! Yes, it hurts! My grip slipped and a scared, angry, large black cockatoo bit my thumb. No fuss was needed, but unfortunately, I had to do an incident report and get it dressed. Later on, whilst in the office filling out the paperwork, my supervisor came over to me and asked me 'how I could avoid not being bitten next time'. WTF! I said, jokingly, 'F**k off! I have caught up many of these birds and this is the first time one has got me.' I told him there is no way you can avoid it, apart from not working with animals. 'You should know that, boss,' I said. He laughed and said, 'Point taken and only you would be so direct and make sure you keep that thumb covered whilst working.'

Sometimes, bites and scratches can lead to infection or zoonotic disease. Applying first aid, a lot of washing of hands and use of sanitizer gel is necessary. Some Zookeepers use gloves, but we personally do not and find it unhelpful because wearing protective gloves for catching up animals can make it difficult to feel the animal and to adjust your restraining techniques for holding an animal safely. It's up to the individual to follow the guidelines and what they feel is appropriate to their experience.

As responsible Zookeepers, we need to keep our tetanus vaccination up. Often, we will build up a better immunity by working with animals. Some Zookeepers working with primates, bats, etc. will need to have yearly TB, hepatitis and rabies injections. We can also worm ourselves once a year, but it's not necessary.

I have noticed over the years that Zookeepers receive common injuries because it's a physical occupation, so care must always be taken. I was trained to lift and move items, animals, stockfeed in the appropriate techniques and to call upon the team when possible. Climbing a ladder is often necessary, so pairing up is compulsory for this duty. Back and shoulder injuries are common with Zookeepers, so like all occupations we need to practice good health and safety, and I was told from the start, there is nothing to prove when it comes to brute strength. Work smarter, as there are no extra points for trying to be a cart horse when working in this field. For our own wellbeing, being fit and looking after yourself and building up some strength for this position is certainly helpful to deliver our duties in a better manner.

At some point, I was getting allergies; an occupational hazard. I started to show symptoms of being allergic to mealworms, which are used to feed out to animals. Mealworms are popular with many animals in zoos. Oh dear! My face blew up and I couldn't see out of my swollen eyes. It was sore and not a pretty sight. I took antihistamine tablets, but it did not always relieve this condition. I was not alone with this reaction. Other long-term Zookeepers also got this allergy, so I had to limit my handling of the mealworms, which was inconvenient at times.

Another rather funny allergy that I developed was when I got swollen lips whilst working closely with koalas and kangaroos. It was an instant botox look! Handling a lot of koalas, sitting on my hip and close to my face meant the fur and odour of eucalyptus was very close. I'm not sure why it caused me to have a reaction, but it did, so I had to take medication to take the swelling down, but it was worth it, having the opportunity to gain cuddles whilst working with an iconic Australian species like the koala.

All Zookeepers work in dirty, dusty environments so dust allergies can also occur. Many Zookeepers that work with hay and straw, usually on the exotic section, can often develop an allergy reaction from 'hay mites' that cause hives which are very sore to work with. This is not a good symptom to have as you will be working closely with these types of food or bedding.

Animals in zoos do escape. When you work with animals, they will escape at any opportunity, so there is no room for error. Zookeepers need to secure their animals, then check and triple check them. Most dangerous animals are locked away at night to prevent escapes. Bad weather, causing trees to fall and fences to be destroyed, is a big problem, so if the animals are locked away overnight, the grounds need to be checked in the morning before they are let out again.

When a team of Zookeepers and I were working hard to improve the rundown zoo in the UK. We had to work fast to repair and replace new structures that had rotted over the years, like fencing and slides. Unfortunately, one night, a wolf escaped from its fragile enclosure. Yes, the Curator's nightmare had happened. On this particular morning, the weather was cold and very foggy and just getting light enough to see as I arrived around 7.30am. I went straight to the office to work with the Curator for a while when I answered an outside phone call from a local. The guy on the phone was working a few kilometres away on some machinery in a quarry. He was a bit anxious and asked me if we had lost a wolf. I quickly informed the Curator, and a head count was made whilst I kept the guy on the line. Confirmation was made that yes, one of the wolves, a young alpha male, was not counted for. I quickly gave instructions to the quarry worker to keep safe and stay in the machinery. Approximately 10 minutes later, the trained and armed Zookeepers plus the outside vet travelled to the area to dart and re-catch the wolf and bring it back to the zoo. The quarry worker certainly had a story to tell his family when he got home safely that evening.

Media got wind of the story and called, trying to get an update, but all information was withheld to keep the situation under control and maintain calmness. Unfortunately, the new owner of the zoo did not understand that an animal escape could effectively stop the zoo getting its licence back and so the story needed to be kept out of the media. But as a journalist himself, he thought all media was good media and continued to speak with them. The Zookeepers and the Curator certainly did not agree and took the escape very seriously.

We managed to control the situation professionally. The wolf was returned to the pack safely, and all were counted for. We felt relief on the catch up and the wolves were put into a more secure enclosure. After this escape, we called in a professional wolf specialist to visit the pack to find out more about the dynamics. He studied the wolves and their behaviour by staying in the enclosure with them, which we all found fascinating. This real situation was not covered in the film *We Bought a Zoo* that went to air a few years later. Unfortunately, this was not an isolated case. The next situation was definitely a serious one for us all involved.

Now moving animals is always a big event; but moving a tiger is a massive event. With much nervous anticipation in the air, the team gathered to commence the sedation, crating and move of a tiger who was on her way to France. As it transpired, she had a safe journey and quickly settled into a huge paddock in a woodland. After a successful introduction to a suitable male, she had cubs. So, on paper, a successful story. The events of the morning that started her journey were not so easily romanticized.

First thing in the morning, the Vet and Curator gathered the team for a brief, and roles were allocated. The Vet and the two first-response lads went into the tiger house where the tiger had been shut in her den, completely unaware what was about to happen: it's quite hard to tell a tiger that they are about to embark on a journey to a better life.

The Vet produced the dart, and the Curator successfully darted the anaesthetic into the tiger's hip. After some time, she became drowsy but didn't go down and sleep. A second dart was administered, and she got steadily more groggy. Now she was down, lying in her den, and appeared to be unconscious.

On the Vet and Curator's nod, two of the team entered the den with the intention to manoeuvre the tiger so she could be lowered onto a blanket and then be stretchered out to the transport crate. The lads made their way around the tiger, and directly opposite the door to the den with the tiger lying between the door and them, they realised that her eyes were open, and she was 'tracking' them. Both froze as the tiger snarled. The tiger house had a passageway too narrow to push a wheelbarrow down and the plan had been to carry the tiger out of the den, along the passageway and down the hill to a crate which was already in the van: doors open, ready to receive a tiger. This tiger, however, was now sitting up in her den, staring at the two keepers who were frozen against the wall of the den in front of her. The vet reached through the safety bars of the den and administered a third dose of anaesthetic with a prod stick. After some snarling and what seemed like a – very – long – time; the tiger laid down and made snoring sounds.

With unknown human-strength the two lads picked up the tiger and carried her through the door of the den and onto the blanket. On landing on the ground, the tiger sat bolt upright and snarled at the lads again. Terrified, the two keepers backed into the den, lying down so they could brace the door shut with their feet. The door's bolt was, of course, on the outside of the door, right by the tiger's nose. The corridor, which had moments before been filled with people, emptied in split seconds and the door slammed and bolted shut. Leaving only a tiger staring at two keepers, both of which were more humble than they have ever previously been or would likely ever be in their lives.

The main door creaked, and the barrel of a dart gun poked through the crack, shooting a fourth dose of anaesthetic into the tiger. As the tiger nudged the door to her den against the feet of the two lads, she became groggy and after some time, she lay down. Without discussing it, the two keepers were out of that den, and had the tiger dragged down the corridor of the tiger house with the only aim of getting her securely and safely in that travel crate with the door firmly shut! The team rallied around, and hands appeared grabbing the blanket. As a team, we carried the tiger down the hill towards the van, adrenaline pumping. Everyone hoped that this would be it: we'd get her in and then have the biggest team sigh of relief. Half-way, the tiger's tail snaked up around the Curator's leg, and he called for everyone to freeze. In panic, several of the team dropped their hold of the blanket, and in plonking her to the ground, the tiger sat up again. Two of the team threw themselves onto her back. The theory here is that if an animal is heavily sedated and has awake moments, heavy pressure to their back can (it is an unfortunate phrase) 'knock-them-out' again.

As the team recoiled in fear to the confines of the narrow path which happened to be between Tiger Rock and the African lion enclosure, the fully grown male lion threw himself at the fence, charging the team that had recoiled to that side of the path. At the same time, the tiger that remained in Tiger Rock threw herself at the fence to attack the team that had recoiled to that side of the path.

Both sides of the path were being simultaneously attacked, completely sandwiching the team between an angry male lion and an angry tiger. And in the middle of all this commotion, a groggy tiger stood up and shook two people off her back as if to say, "Get the f**k off me!"

What followed was terrifyingly mesmerizing. The Curator and the marksman had an eye-to-eye conversation about whether he should shoot this tiger who was now walking down the path, or not. The risk to the tiger was fatal. The risk to the people she was pacing past was fatal. In the passing seconds of that last hour, it really seemed as though there couldn't be a good outcome.

The team froze where they stood against fences with a roaring lion and snarling tiger while the groggy yet quite alert tiger padded down the hill. With a shotgun cocked and aimed at her, she padded to the van, swirled a full 360 degrees and collapsed. The team cautiously approached the seemingly unconscious tiger, one of whom actually sat stroking her for a moment. In a heartbeat, the rest of the team then grabbed the tiger by whatever they could and shoved her into the crate. The vet administered a reversal drug, not that that seemed to be required from what we'd just experienced: three times. The crate door was screwed shut with as many screws as we could find. The van doors shut, locked and the wide-eyed French boys that were doing the transport had hands shaken and sent on their way!

Years later, revisiting this experience, the emotions of what could have been are quite overwhelming. Not only could, or indeed should, someone have been killed that day: that tiger had a rubbish experience. And that's not fair, the tiger deserved better and better wasn't delivered by the people who had influence over that process. It transpired on investigation that the Vet had used a horse sedative, but this was a big cat and not a horse, it hadn't had the desired effect.

In hindsight, 18 years after the event, we can marvel that one man in a position of authority made some bad decisions, and those decisions could have cost several lives and indeed the life of a tiger who was unaware of what was happening. As it turned out, she had a great life.

My mate, one of the Zookeepers who jumped onto the back of the tiger, refreshed my memory by writing this scary event up for me. Luckily the outcome was safe, and his great Zookeeper/Bird Keeper skills has carried on with his passion for setting up his own bird garden in Scotland which houses many species of birds that are endangered or threatened in natural habitat enclosures We both hope to make a visit next year to see this great set up and share sometime again chatting over zoo life.

As mentioned, coming from the UK meant I did not have the exposure to snakes growing up, so they were not my favourite animals. But whilst living here, I have also realised a lot of born and bred Australians have not been exposed to many snakes either.

When I started at the zoo in Australia, I was hoping I would not be put onto this section and, luckily, I got away with it for years. But eventually I was put in the reptile section, and this was a new challenge that I finally embraced. I informed my Senior Zookeeper that I had a lot of skills working with a variety of animals, but certainly none with snakes.

Bugger, I could not hide from it! I received the training to work with these snakes and started to appreciate these reptiles and thought I was getting over my fear. That was until the Head Keeper of the Reptile section wanted to train me to be number two Zookeeper when servicing venomous snakes.

The experienced trained venomous Zookeeper always needs to be assisted by another Zookeeper when servicing the venomous snakes' enclosure. This morning before the zoo opened for the day, I was instructed to stand next to the venomous snakes Zookeeper whilst the glass door was opened. My heart was pounding as the two very active venomous snakes were prominent. Then my biggest fear came true. One of the snakes went onto the ground and slivered towards my feet. F...k! My flight mode kicked in, and I ran and climbed up the nearest ladder 15 metres away... *oh dear, not my finest moment!*

Let's say that for the rest of the month, the reptile Zookeepers took the piss out of me. I was retrained and tested many times with this duty, so next time I was needed, I would feel confident to stay and assist. My heart never did stop pounding whilst performing this duty.

Little did I know that a few months later, I would cycle fast to be one of the first Zookeepers that arrived at an emergency code call on the two-way. Another Zookeeper was bitten by a large python snake and the Zookeeper's arm was being wrapped around and squeezed by this snake, needing urgent help to remove the snake off the arm. I managed to help a Senior Zookeeper, Mike, to remove this big snake, allowing the Zookeeper to be freed and taken to hospital to be checked over. With training and confidence under another more experienced Senior Reptile Keeper, I managed to perform this emergency without any hesitancy.

We are all aware that zoos in Australia have certainly had their fair share of animal attacks on Zookeepers over the years. In 2020, a Zookeeper was attacked by two lions. The majestic creatures viciously attacked her, leaving her physically and emotionally scarred. This Zookeeper was lucky to be alive and managed to return to work as a Lion Zookeeper at another zoo after full recovery. Another Zookeeper was attacked by a crocodile during a feeding show at a zoo with the public watching on. Fortunately, this Zookeeper managed to escape the hold and recovered. Certainly not something we want to witness. Another horrific attack happened at a zoo in Austria where a Zookeeper applied insect repellent on a rhino. The Zookeeper was crushed to death and the Rhino seriously injured her husband who attempted to save her. The zoo had not had any incidents during its 30 years of operation. An incident that can happen just like that and is shocking. Zookeepers must never have the opinion that it will not happen to us. In fact, the opposite is needed to keep us on our toes. Duty of care is necessary at all times, but as Zookeepers we know these incidents can and will happen.

What we have noticed is that most zoos' management often avoid speaking out on these situations, and they will certainly not take any responsibility for these accidents. The line 'Zookeeper error' is often used.

Animals getting out is scary. If a gorilla gets out and meets a Zookeeper, they will charge at you and knock you down. A gorilla is up to 20 times stronger than a human male. If a chimpanzee gets out, they will run, jump on you, bite, scream and attack you. They are up to 5 times stronger than a human male. An orangutan is up to 7 times stronger than a human male. If an orangutan gets out, they will slowly bite and pull pieces off you, watching on at each act to see what happens, a slow painful experience or death. Amazing information to us, but maybe not for everyone.

I have witnessed some minor but damaging animal attacks, including cockatoos flying towards a face, biting and causing plenty of damage, a gannet sea bird using its sharp beak to stab a Zookeeper's eye and a resident large kangaroo attack at a wildlife rehabilitation centre. A long-term experienced volunteer that fed the Roo on a regular basis was suddenly attacked. This person went to hospital with over 100 stitches from bites

IT'S A DANGEROUS JOB   151

and scratches. When you are a Zookeeper, we know what the high-risk animals are and follow strict health and safety protocols that are set out. We are trained and signed off to work with these animals, and only these Zookeepers can enter and service the animals. Other Zookeepers or any staff or volunteers that have not been trained to work with these animals should never enter their enclosure or service these animals.

Mike, as a Senior Zookeeper, has had to address safety issues regarding free ranging kangaroos for the visitors to walk amongst, even touching and taking photos without supervision. It was a major accident waiting to happen. At one small zoo, he walked into a situation where over the years, the general public had been injured, and within the first two weeks of him starting, a little girl nearly lost her eye from a kangaroo attack. Mike had to recommend and convince management that he needed to reorganize and make this potentially dangerous situation safe for everyone. He achieved this by building an enclosed fenced off area so the kangaroos could feel safe and have their own space, and the visitors could watch and touch at a safe distance. As Zookeepers we should never become complacent with any animal, especially when mixing animals with the public.

Another incident at a large zoo in WA was when a child jumped on a kangaroo which was lying down, causing rib injuries to the kangaroo which led to the animal being put down. For the safety of the animal and the visitors, a barrier is really more suitable.

I always remember when I was around 8 years old at an animal circus in the UK. I went to see a large male kangaroo boxing with a human for entertainment. Yes, back then, it was called entertainment. Even then, as a kid, I did not like to see it but remember seeing the pure strength and full respect owed to this unique animal, the most famous marsupial and icon of Australia.

As Zookeepers, people will often ask us, "Have you got any animal escape stories?" In this world there certainly are stories, some very sad and some end happily.

One of the sad ones was at a Primate Rescue Centre I visited in Spain, which was delivering great work, rescuing all sorts of primates that were pets or performed in the circus. (Yes, animal circuses still exist in some countries.) It was very inspiring to see the rescue centre's amazing work, and the facilities were brilliant. I have worked for a short time with primates, and they are way too smart and cunning for me to want to work with permanently, but so many people feel the opposite to me. A few months after visiting the Rescue Centre, after getting to know the Zookeepers and the animals, I heard tragic news of chimpanzees escaping due to a fallen tree. They became frightened whilst out of their large natural enclosure. Straight from the Zookeeper mouths, they informed me that they worked so hard frantically trying to get them securely back into their safe enclosure, but unfortunately, the chimps kept on running to a small nearby town. The police took over and shot the chimpanzees. This would have been a Zookeeper's worst nightmare, a mental fuck up imprinted on your brain forever.

As at any zoo, there have been some close calls at the large zoo I worked at in WA. Any animals that manage to escape from their enclosure on your sections are treated very seriously and you can lose your job, so it's a high priority to always lock, check and recheck your animals. A code call was made when an adult female orangutan climbed out of her enclosure to collect her baby, which had fallen out of the enclosure into the gardens below. An orangutan is classed as a dangerous animal. She retrieved her baby and climbed back into the enclosure. This took about 15 minutes whilst visitors walked away under the guidance of staff. It was a shock for everyone, and the incident was treated with high urgency, as it could have been very dangerous. On this occasion, it went well for everyone. The public did manage to get footage of this situation, and the media covered it.

At the same zoo, there was a serious incident at the elephant enclosure where a code was called for a dangerous animal. Mike was now working on the Australian Section and out on a field trip in the Pilbara when he heard that the male elephant had tried to escape out of his enclosure. The large male elephant was in musk and decided to show his strength by pushing down the fence and ignoring instruction from the Zookeeper. This was a highly dangerous situation. The zoo was evacuated whilst the situation was controlled. A male elephant in the musk mode is always dangerous, but one out running around the zoo would be deadly.

It's a Competitive Job

Many Zookeepers start out as volunteers in zoos. As I have mentioned, it's a competitive world to work in, so gaining whatever experience you can is necessary. Zoos depend on volunteers to help. These volunteers can bring in other life skills to the zoo. Good volunteers are valuable to both the Zookeepers and the animals, and they should always be respected as part of the team. Not all Zookeepers show this respect, and we both find it crazy and very disappointing. Some of our kind volunteers, whilst working in zoos, have become our friends in the outside world.

Once you are a contract Zookeeper, it doesn't always mean working hard will gain you more contracts. It doesn't go on merit, or first in, or how much loyalty is shown as to who gets a position. This is where it can cause morale issues amongst all Zookeepers, especially in Western Australia, as there are not many places to find work in this field. The clear structure we saw in place was respected when we started, but nowadays it's not so prominent. We had to participate in achievements to go up a level; it was not automatic. This on-the-job training was a good system, covering all areas, and Zookeepers gained more confidence getting ticked off as they went along in their training. On our journey, it took a Zookeeper between 6 to 10 years to achieve a Senior role. A good organisation will recognise relevant experience in this field, and a higher position will only be given if proven. Everyone started at level 1.1, level 1.2, or level 1.3. Once you gained a Zookeeping certificate, you could go up to level 2. Level 3 up was a Senior Zookeeper.

Now we hear you can only achieve a Senior Zookeeper position when it becomes available, then apply with the relevant experience to get this position. Colleagues have told us that Zookeepers who now have many years of experience (10 years plus) though not officially a Senior Zookeeper will still fulfil senior roles if needed on a particular day. I always practiced the ranking system in zoos, *'a chain of commands'*, which should be respected. Not all Zookeepers did this, and it caused a lot of grief if you do not practice this. We have both received this poor action. One that stood out for Mike was when he was the Head Elephant Keeper. At this particular time, this section was short of staff, and it was well known in the zoo that they were working long hours under extreme pressure. There was an opportunity to gain a permanent position on this section, but I felt the elephants were not my area and also, you need to be the right person to work with these amazing large animals and to be committed for years to gain their confidence and respect. Disappointingly, other people did not take this into consideration; they wanted to be a Zookeeper whatever. This led to many unsuitable people applying for this position.

Back 20 years ago, whilst Mike was trying to train a new inexperienced Zookeeper, he noticed right from the beginning she was showing plenty of nerves, and not a confident person in general.

This was a big concern when working with dangerous animals. Mike tried to reassure her by saying, "stand tall, use your voice, deeply, use your balls." I would not have a problem with this comment, totally understanding what the Head Keeper was saying, but this Zookeeper went straight to the next in line boss and made a complaint! Seriously, you are working with extremely dangerous animals, and this was good advice and should have just been taken on board and not be so precious in this dangerous environment.

This is a common terminology expression to use a deeper tone of voice, which is very important when training and working with animals in a free contact situation. TV presenters even say this phrase these days! What has the world come to with this constant ridiculous woke behaviour? And, speak with the person if you are uncomfortable with anything, don't run to the boss. So from my experience it is obvious that Zookeepers would/should know not to run and bother the Head Keeper or the Curator with any animal issues or on the ground exhibit/staff issues if they are not the Zookeeper's immediate contact. Our first port of call is the Senior Zookeeper or the next experienced Zookeeper. Communication should be kept open always.

As Zookeepers we receive formal training for many years through mentors. People entering the world with a Zoology degree or Vet Nursing qualification is a bonus and certainly offers some background and help, but it does not make you a Zookeeper, just like a Zookeeper entering a vet practice, does not make you a Vet Nurse.

We should not be in competition but join forces and be united in our work. We have a day to be proud and celebrate; it's International Zookeeper Day.

The Underbelly of the Zoo World

Over the years parents, kids, students and others have asked us if Zookeeping is a good profession. We have asked ourselves on many occasions, 'if we knew more about this journey, would we have chosen to work with animals or be a Zookeeper in a zoo?'

At the beginning of our career, we would have said yes, but now, knowing the pain, stress, and bullshit you have to take, it's questionable at times. There is a lot of *'good, bad, and ugly'* in being a Zookeeper. Zookeepers are, for the most part, chronically underpaid and there are limited opportunities for promotion available in this field. But when you choose to be responsible for captive husbandry of a large range of native and exotic animals on display to the public, it always comes back to the love of animals.

Being a Zookeeper is certainly not for everyone, and it's not like being a lawyer or teacher. If you do not like the zoo or wildlife park you are working in, you cannot up and go somewhere else just like that. *After reading this book, maybe you'll be able to answer this for yourself, whether this is a good profession for you or someone you know.*

It's rarely the animals that are the problem. Let's talk about break-ins, thieves, idiots and animal murders.

Zookeepers have to deal with thieves and idiots on a daily basis. They will often feed the animals with the wrong food, climb into enclosures and try to steal animals. People drop their hats or sunglasses whilst viewing, others accidentally drop their kids into enclosures! As we all know, this can lead to humans being hurt or killed. All this puts the animal at risk too. At no fault of their own, some animals have been shot and killed or hurt due to the selfish act of the human not respecting their home.

Since mobile phones have been around, some people act in a silly manner. They go crazy trying to grab a selfie with all sorts of animals. This encourages people to get up close to animals, which leads to the public climbing onto walls or into enclosures, putting themselves as well as the animals and keepers at high risk. Then some f...king idiots fall into enclosures. Yes, fall in! A famous story was when a boy fell into a gorilla enclosure back in the 70s in the UK. This came to world attention and ended with a good result. The kid slid from his parent's shoulder and landed semi-unconscious into the gorilla enclosure. The public kept calm, and the silverback (alpha male gorilla) was calm, holding the kid to protect him from the female gorillas whilst everyone watched on. The Zookeepers managed to get all the gorillas into the night quarters, rescuing the child unharmed and that boy has grown up to tell the story. *This enclosure was in the zoo that I previously mentioned, where a large silverback gorilla on loan from Melbourne welcomed me with delight each morning.*

There was a similar story more recently in the USA, but this time there was not a happy ending. The same happened—a child fell into a gorilla enclosure, but the public screamed and overreacted at the male gorilla who dragged the kid around. Not knowing the animal's behaviour, the furore alarmed the troop, and panic set in. The Zookeepers could not get the gorillas secured inside and the firearms team had to shoot this incredible creature. As a Zookeeper, I could see from the media coverage that it was a hasty decision and a very sad one. The Zookeepers would be devastated by this incident. Our duty as Zookeepers is to get the animals locked away into the night quarters to prevent the attack, but these are unknown humans in their territory, and the animals will usually harm or kill whatever enters their home. We understand it's a natural response to defend their territory.

Break-ins are the Zookeeper's nightmare. It's very stressful for the Zookeepers, not knowing if the animals they are responsible for have been hurt, killed or stolen. Zoos around the world get broken into, so it's very important that the security is high to make sure the animals in our care are protected. Many animals are stolen and never seen again, getting a high price for their species on the black market.

The next story is too much for a Zookeeper to handle. While working overseas, I witnessed a disgusting news story of some young adults that had been drinking and taking drugs. They climbed into the City Zoo and cut all the penguins' heads off for fun. The people who do this kind of act could be under the influence of drugs, or just cruel, insane bastards. Some of these penguins were terribly injured but still alive when the Zookeepers arrived. This would have been so horrific for the Zookeepers to deal with.

There are people out there that will break in and release animals, like birds, and these animals will not survive out in the wild. Here in Australia, a zoo was broken into where many birds were slaughtered, and all the Zookeepers and staff came to work to find this disgusting and pointless act of cruelty.

Reptiles and exotic birds appear to be the most common targets to be stolen. Whilst working in zoos in the UK, though security was good, endangered birds and monkeys were stolen overnight by professional collectors. Most of these animals die from the horrible ordeal or end up found in drug houses. I am aware of this as a friend who was an RSPCA Officer found and rescued some monkeys being kept in a room under terrible conditions. These were the same monkeys that were stolen weeks before from a zoo.

Later, on my return to Western Australia, I saw on the news that some radiated tortoises were stolen and only found/returned because the story was leaked out to the media, exposing the situation. This led to the general public helping to locate these stolen animals within days. I was informed that the zoo's management expressed to all current Zookeepers that they were not happy that the story leaked out and appeared to be more concerned about that than getting these animals back safe and sound, and not just dumped anywhere to die. *Oh dear, I wonder how this story got out*?

It was an ex-Zookeeper (me) now a member of the public. I had raised the questionable security risk of this enclosure when I was working on this round years before, so I was not surprised this had happened. There is terrible grief for Zookeepers when animals are stolen.

Another weird story was when a wild animal stole a zoo animal. I was working and listening to my two-way, and I heard the code that a baby meerkat had been seen stolen by a crow from an outside enclosure. It flew off, but luckily dropped the meerkat quickly onto the main grass area. The visitor saw it happen and found the baby meerkat, located a Zookeeper and this little one was vet checked and returned to his enclosure with its mob. It's something we can't always prevent but a good ending due to the visitor noticing and helping.

If an emergency code call is made for a fire that has broken out in a zoo, the Zookeepers will need to hose down enclosures, put reticulation on, move animals in direct threat of the fire or smoke and follow animal section policies. A Senior Zookeeper, Header Keeper, Curator, will be allocated to coordinate the animal evacuation and two-way silence is necessary to follow instructions. Zookeepers are responsible for the animals and will and want to stay as long as it is safe to do so.

Another harrowing experience is public suicides in zoos. Australia has not been exempt from this. Suicide attempts by the general public climbing into enclosures at zoos is a harsh act as it puts everyone at risk, including us Zookeepers. In the past, people have deliberately climbed into a dangerous animal enclosure as a suicide act, creating a very messy environment for everyone involved.

Here at a large zoo in WA, there have been incidents over the years where members of the public have climbed into enclosures. In 1950, a young woman was found mauled to death, and a year later, a young man was found dead in the same enclosure, but killed by different lions. These enclosures had an 18 foot fence, but from the deceased bodies, it was found that they were probably conscious when attacked. It was confirmed that climbing of the fence is characteristic of a person suffering from mental instability. Persons in such a condition are capable of performing feats of strength and agility considered extremely difficult for even the best trained athletes.

Later in the 1970s, a young aggressive man under the influence of drugs climbed into the polar bears enclosure during the day and received a slow, agonizing death of being pulled and ripped apart in front of about 30 people. We both knew one keeper that participated in the rescue and witnessed this horrific sight on that day. Sadly, in 2023, in Germany, a young woman had lost her teacher's job and was going through a terrible time, and her mental health was suffering. This woman climbed into a polar bear enclosure, fell into the pool and was attacked by two polar bears. It took 7 Zookeepers to scare the polar bears into their night quarters to rescue the women. This woman received terrible bite wounds over her but was still alive to rush to the hospital. This is a very painful death, and the risk is very high to everyone.

Zookeepers and Mental Health

Working with animals is an interesting path to take, but it can be filled with heartaches as well as joy. Every day of the year, animals need to be looked after. This job is physically and mentally demanding and it can be tough. It delivers a low pay, with long hours. It's a lifestyle. Yes, it can be so rewarding, but also very depressing, causing many people around the world working in this animal industry, conservation, farms and vets to develop depression and anxiety, knowing the species they are working with may become extinct, whatever the good intentions are to save it. Non-animal people will not understand why people working with animals get so worked up. Only people in this field with the same drive and passion will relate to the stress it can cause. Mental health has come to light in the last few years, which is a good thing. It has been shown that vets and farmers who work with animals are the highest occupations for mental health issues, leading to suicides. Mournfully, I have also heard of Wildlife Careers driven by passion can become overwhelmed. With the influx of animals that need help, dealing with deaths, the politics of the system, the human population impacting on this planet can be too much at times, causing suicides in this field. We both understand the pressure, isolation and hard decision-making that is involved whilst working with animals, which can have a very detrimental impact on mental health.

When I started out as a Zookeeper, I was shocked when I heard about a very dedicated Head Zookeeper at this zoo, who had recently taken his own life whilst working with primates. They are a very emotional animal to work with; they are so like humans. The death of this person was very sad and distressing to hear about, especially at the start of my new journey.

Years later, I experienced it again, this time working closely with the Zookeeper in question. When I got back to my position from being overseas, things were a little different. This Zookeeper, who I'll call Sheila, was now working on our section. Sheila had gone through a hard time and was suffering severe anxiety and depression. She had been transferred to another section, which had a very bad impact on her mental health. Sheila was an experienced but fairly young Zookeeper and had been hand-raising a primate baby. Her Curator decided she wasn't going to raise the baby anymore, which was a massive loss. At the morning meeting, I tried to lift the mood by letting the Zookeepers know that her Curator at our zoo had a rubbish reputation on the other side of the world of being a 'dickhead'. All the Zookeepers laughed, and I was put with Sheila for the day because some of the Zookeepers commented that I had made her smile and laugh for the first time in months, but all I could see was a very sad person. I worked along the side of this once inspired Zookeeper all day and at one point, I offered to take a photo with one of the animals for her record. She quickly replied, "No thank you, no photos." At the time, I thought it was an unusual reply. The following morning, before I arrived at the zoo, my Curator called me as he had done with the other Zookeepers to inform us that Sheila had sadly taken her own life overnight. I was horrified, so in shock. I felt terrible that this person was suffering so much, and her loss had made her unwell. It certainly made me realise how fragile life can be.

Now experiencing all this, it has given me empathy for all people going through rough times in their everyday life and I can see that everyone is vulnerable to their mental health declining.

Unfortunately, from both our years of zoo experience we have seen Zookeepers being treated poorly, like being taken off sections where their passion is. Their skills, knowledge and emotional attachment are controlled by management for whatever reason, and this can be very dangerous. We have witnessed the impact on the Zookeeper, animal and their family. We believe some management actions should be monitored, and mental health and wellbeing need to be taken more seriously in the zoo world.

And it doesn't stop there. Sadly, we knew a good elephant keeper who was brought up with elephants in Malaysia. He relocated the elephants and got the opportunity to come to Australia to settle the elephants in their new home. We both worked with this Zookeeper; he always worked hard, went above and beyond as a great Zookeeper for years on the elephant section. Mike learnt a lot from him, but suddenly he was moved off and put on to another section, due to a conflict with another Zookeeper. With this type of transfer, the animals suffer as well as the Zookeeper and the whole section. This management decision had a serious impact on this Zookeeper's mental health status. Later, when he left the zoo to work in another field, it was a huge reason for his attempt at suicide, which saddened us. We both knew that this Zookeeper's skills were a massive loss due to this act, and maybe all this could have been handled with a more positive outcome. Over the years, many Zookeepers have left the zoo or been terminated, from either unfair dismissals, sacked, constructive dismissals, injuries, or sickness by management they have been damaged by. Sorry to say, but it's not uncommon to hear this story in the zoo world (some terrible management decisions).

Working in the zoo world can be mentally challenging. Most of your network of friends will work with animals and will understand this environment. Working in conservation can be a depressing field. Knowing that there is no decent habitat left for the species you are looking after to survive in the wild is demoralising.

Fortunately, I had never been exposed to mental health issues growing up, but in more recent years, I have certainly suffered from anxiety and depression, which I am open about. I never thought this would happen to me, but it did further down the track of my life journey at the end of my career as a Zookeeper. I asked my physiologist why this has happened to me. It was possible that being sensitive to the environment, noticing things, caring for animals and the planet can all create anxiety in some individuals. Often people we have met say to us, 'how is it you see and rescue so many animals? We never see them on the road.' Maybe it's because we are more aware of our environment and so see it.

The media and other organisations may speak out, saying that they are aware of mental health and support people struggling, but in our opinion, it's lip service and bullshit. I was shocked when I eventually had to put in a Workers Compensation claim regarding work related mental health issues which are hard to prove. With evidence that this career has contributed to the decline of mental health, even lawyers in this field say it needs to be changed for this condition to be taken seriously. Workplaces like zoos need to be accountable for this unhealthy environment that can be created or present for Zookeepers to work in.

However, it was animals that helped me overcome it. Yes, animals came to the rescue with my mental health; my own dog. When the anxiety started, I had just got a 14-week-old black kelpie. He appeared to recognise my anxiety, which led to panic attacks, and he supported me. At one stage, before managing my panic attacks with medication, my amazing dog (usually a working breed) would comfort me whilst having these episodes. I certainly did not feel alone. Having your best friend next to you with its unconditional love is massive for mental health. This experience guided me to become involved with assistance dogs, service dogs and therapy dogs.

Under guidance, I trained my own young kelpie and then a certified assistance dog. A trainer passed him to be qualified to be my assistance dog, which I then carried an ID. My dog was amazing, and the confidence I got from having him with me is hard to express, and I am so grateful.

All trained service dogs are incredible. They can be different breeds, helping members of society to function. With having mental health issues, I've acquired high empathy in an area that I wasn't exposed to before. Having my dog with me helped my life and was a big contribution in managing my anxiety. Getting involved with assistance dogs made me appreciate all the great dogs offering support to their humans. These dogs put themselves on the line in wars or to protect us in normal life as police dogs, rescue dogs, security and so many more services, as well as the connection they provide to us all. Once you have a dog, you will never go back to living without your most loyal friend.

Whenever I read sayings like the ones below, it always makes me smile, and I'm so thankful to be surrounded by animals (and not so many people!).

"Our perfect companions never have fewer than four feet." Colette

"The purity of a person's heart can be quickly measured by how they regard animals." Theophile Gautier

"Until one has loved an animal a part of one's soul remains unawakened." Anatole France

"The love for all living creatures is the most noble attribute of man." Charles Darwin

"If having a soul means being able to feel love and loyalty and gratitude, then animals are better off than a lot of humans." James Herriot

"Animals are such agreeable friends – they ask no questions, they pass no criticisms." George Eliot

"For an animal person, an animal-less home is no home at all." Cleveland Amory

"The greatness of a nation can be judged by the way its animals are treated." Mahatma Gandhi

"The greatness of animals is that they are just themselves." Alice Walker

Humans Behaving Badly

Humans can be exposed in a bad light, and as Zookeeper you sometimes see the public behaving badly. It's important that we make ourselves present in the zoo to monitor the animals, particularly if the animals under your care live in an interactive enclosure where the public may be behaving badly. A Zookeeper needs to interact with the visitors at all times. We have found this to be important, as unfortunately the general public have no idea that walking off the path (*even though there are signs saying 'please keep on the path stay off animal refuge'*) can cause stress, and even death to the animals.

The visitors have been known to chase kangaroos for selfie photos in off-limit safety areas with shelter for the animals. This act causes stress for the animal, but also a serious health and safety situation for the customer. Mike had to erect a small fence in a large zoo for the kangaroos, as they were getting injured from the public. In another zoo, he had to stop the free-range kangaroos and build a new area for them so they were protected and could relax because some visitors just do not respect the animals' space.

This means us Zookeepers can relax from customers getting injured from the interaction. Free-range can only work if there is a trained, full-time volunteer or Zookeeper to monitor animals the whole time. I have personally experienced parents and children walking off the path, right up to the feeding area of adorable guinea pigs, grabbing them for the kids to hold even though it's very clear and says *'keep on path and do not pick up the guinea pigs'*. These animals could have easily been trodden on or dropped without supervision, but for some reason, people think animals are there for their entertainment and will grab and touch without respect.

Some of this bad behaviour means other visitors miss out. A lovely lady we knew donated some peacock eggs. We incubated the eggs, then hand raised the peacock chicks. They were so popular, the public loved them, but it took one out-of-control kid chasing the peacocks. When the peacock flew up and away, it scared and scratched the child. This incident was blown up because management allowed the media to cover the story without responding. The unfair coverage from this particular member of the public led to management (who were acting without understanding animal behaviour) to take the peacocks off display. Now everyone misses out on these popular stunning birds due to one selfish action of the general public. Plenty of visitors to the park loved the spectacular natural beauty they displayed. These birds found a loving life out on acreage, to be appreciated in their pure beauty. Peacocks are free range in the majority of zoos around the world. The general public needs to be aware that zoos are not parks for people to behave poorly. This is the animals' home and should be respected by all. The challenge for us Zookeepers is to face this on a daily basis.

Maybe we shouldn't laugh, but as Zookeepers we couldn't help but chuckle at these stories. Zoos can be dangerous not for the animals, but from dopey visitors walking around the zoo and getting themselves into trouble. In the UK, an employee was a scarer on Halloween. The Zoo worker terrified a visitor so much that they lashed out in fright, accidentally knocking the worker to the ground, who ended up with a broken wrist and feeling very silly. At another zoo, a visitor in the gift shop ended up with a 3-inch cut to their head after tripping over a large donation box, causing chaos in the shop. What a circus!

All us humans love to watch the funniest animal videos, animal Instagram posts, reels, etc. It's enjoyable for sure. It can bring a big smile to your face. Watching animals chase their owners, play with their owners, even give cuddles to their owners is lovely. Watching roosters and rams chase their owners, lions and chimpanzee babies love their owners, through play, etc. is the best feel-good therapy to view. However, Zookeepers are very much aware of animal behaviour and often see potential animal risk moments way before the average Jo does. Understanding the risk and being cautious is always necessary with any animal. Children and animals should always be monitored at all times for the health and safety of the child and for the well-being of the animal. *This does include your pet dogs and cats. It's not always the animal's error if it attacks. Children and animals should always be supervised.*

Crazy Zookeeper or Not?

Talking about the circus, some people may say that Joe Exotic from *Tiger King* is a crazy Zookeeper or maybe he is not?

Whilst Mike and I watched this series on Netflix during the COVID lock down, we found this coverage to be absorbing. It was based on behind the scenes of some Zookeepers who owned 'big cat zoos' in the USA. It certainly was an eye opener in all ways for the general public, but also to some Zookeepers.

As experienced Zookeepers, we watched the show, knowing that the producers would have taken some of the camera work out of context to make it more shocking to the general public who are not familiar with the zoo world. The owners of the private zoos and wildlife parks certainly took advantage of keen Zookeepers that wanted to work with these amazing but dangerous animals. They thought they had found their dream job, but it was certainly a dirty job, and not in the way of physically clearing up piles of dirt and shit. For us here in Australia, we are at the other end of the scale in not being allowed to own native or exotic animals as pets. It's very difficult to gain permission here in Australia. Where in the USA it appears to be extremely easy for the general public to own animals such as chimps and tigers at a low cost of $3,000. It's madness, and fairly accessible for most people. Maybe this should be looked at to prevent people getting these animals because they want one. The owners of these sanctuaries appear to be egoistic, more like 'Show Ponies' than Zookeepers. There appears to be a market, so these organisations breed and sell the cubs to support the zoo. These Zookeepers were certainly a misfit bunch, which can be a little normal in the zoo world!

This show exposed to the world that America's large population of captive tigers is estimated to be as many as 7,000 of the big cats in the United States today, while only around 5,000 tigers survive in the wild in other countries. This show brings the situation to light, resulting in a good thing, helping scientists in this field. Apparently, over 99 percent of those American tigers live in unaccredited roadside zoos, private residences or sanctuaries. Conservationists have long wondered what types of tigers make up this population and whether their genetic material could help increase the number of tigers in the wild. Scientists are looking into this situation, so this could be a great result for the overcrowded captive tigers to the wild ones that are depleting. I hope that some good results come from this exposure for the splendour of the tiger to continue.

Trafficking

Working with animals means you are exposed to hearing tragic events. When I started out as a trainee Zookeeper, I worked on the bird section where you need to be very observant. The trafficking of Australian birds was brought to my attention. I was not previously aware of this disgusting criminal act.

Traffickers would catch birds from the wild and stuff them in things like plumbing pipes in a suitcase, and as long as one of the birds made it to Europe, USA, etc., then it was financially worth them doing this cruel act. The punishment is low, and the gain is very high, so these people do not care if hundreds of birds die. Recently in the news here in Australia, Wildlife Officers for DBCA had been watching a group of reptile smugglers and finally caught them at the airport with hundreds of bobtails and snakes stolen from the wild. Because reptiles can survive in small dark places, they are easier to smuggle out. Eggs are another one that can be carried on people, and it just takes one endangered egg to make it worthwhile. The fines for these acts need to be taken more seriously to discourage these criminals. I took an interest in this and became aware of undercover wildlife officers who go into dangerous situations, pretending to be potential customers to buy, say a sloth and hopefully catch these people. Just like working with Greenpeace, people put their lives on the line to make changes and it's important that we give them full respect and support. I did consider working for these organisations going undercover, but this was when I was younger and had the energy to commit to such a great but risky cause.

As Zookeepers we need to be aware that trading in exotic pets from foreign countries is a global multi-billion dollar industry, and Australian species are highly sought after. Australia banned the commercial export of all live native animals in 1982. But once wildlife is taken out of the country, these laws no longer apply. Many species can be legally traded without restrictions once they are beyond our borders.

The main International Trade in Endangered Species Wild Fauna and Flora legislation is known as CITES. This is an agreement between 184 governments to ensure international trade in wild animals and plants does not threaten species survival, but apparently Australia needs to update the list of animals on this agreement.

Zookeepers Behaving Badly

After working overseas for approximately 10 years, I had developed my skills in the zoo world and learnt heaps, but I needed to return to Australia. I was really missing the lifestyle of Oz, and it was time to go home. I did not plan to return to work at the original zoo I started at, so I started up my own business, importing a product. However, I still had a lot of friends working at the zoo, and they were short of experienced Zookeepers, so I contacted the Head Keeper and got some work there again. The zoo had not changed much. A few Zookeepers I knew were still around, and some new Zookeepers who were a little unfriendly. This can happen in this industry; there are some shitty Zookeepers out there. All Zookeepers represent our role, and it is bad form to be hostile to other Zookeepers who might be visiting or getting a contract or permanent position at the zoo. I found it hard to see these Zookeepers behave like this—that they are missing out, feeling threatened or not embracing the new. I have seen this 'snake in the grass' behaviour before. It's not necessary and not pleasant to experience. New Senior Zookeepers like me who come onboard should be respected. They are not treading on anyone's feet, and they can offer good advice. Both of us have received hostile behaviour coming into a new zoo. When I gained an overseas Senior Zookeeper position in a highly regarded UK zoo, my first few days were not pleasant. I found other Zookeepers to not be that friendly or obliging. Then I was told the truth. Many other Zookeepers had applied and wanted this position, so they resented me getting it as I was from overseas. This Zookeeper then said, *'but how could we not like you'* and apologized. They appreciated the different skills I was bringing to the section and luckily, we got past that in a few days.

There are Zookeepers and there are *great* Zookeepers. Not all people in this industry maintain a good attitude. For example, we are both a little tired of hearing some Zookeepers 'squeal like a pig', but unfortunately, we have come across this. It's stressful to work with Zookeepers that do not perform all the jobs, who are lazy and pick and choose, then leave the not-so-great duties for others to perform. Complaining can cause other Zookeepers to disrespect you and become a joke with more experienced Zookeepers. As an experienced Zookeeper, I have been frustrated with this attitude and I'm not alone in this. My co-workers have left the unpleasant jobs of taking out old branches that are dry or not dealing with gassing chicks or mice and leaving it for the next Zookeeper. Some Zookeepers think they are above dealing with the rat and mice baits duty, but they are not. As a contractor for many years, some permanent full time Zookeepers were arses taking advantage of the keen contract Zookeepers, leaving us all the crap jobs.

I found some descriptions which go a way to explain some good and some bad behaviours of Zookeepers.

- Zookeepers need to not work like a **'Sloth'**, but work at a good steady pace.

- Zookeepers need to not work like a **'Bat out of hell'**, but work at a good steady pace.

- Zookeepers should not put on the **'Crocodile'** tears and be over-sensitive.

- Zookeepers should not be a **'Weasel'**, no one likes a Zookeeper that acts like a weasel.

- Zookeepers should not be a **'Fair Weather'** Zookeeper, stay out in all weathers with your animals.

- Zookeepers should work like a **Cheetah, Bear, Fox and Lion**. This represents different attributes, roles and styles within a team, and this is very true in the Zookeeper Team.

- Zookeepers should work like a **'Beaver'** or an **'Ant'** in a good hard-working team.

- Zookeepers have some pride and do not play **'Cat and Mouse'** games in zoos.

Unfortunately, there are a lot of cat and mouse games within the zoo world. *Cat and Mouse games, describe behaviour in which someone says or does different things to deceive or control other people to avoid being caught.* Certainly, this behaviour is present in some Zookeepers and management we have had the misfortune to work with.

I would like to continue with embarrassing Zookeeper behaviour. Inexperienced Zookeepers are nicknamed 'Google Zookeepers', using their mobiles to gain information instead of using experienced Zookeepers to answer questions. Experienced Zookeepers have a little chuckle at this, and if we are noticing, then maybe the public is too, and laugh like a kookaburra sitting on the fence. As experienced Zookeepers, we find this behaviour ridiculous and any credibility you may have had will go if you get caught doing this. Most Google Zookeepers will get it wrong and show themselves up to the detriment of the animals. From our experience, self-teaching is not going to 'hack it' in this jungle and you will end up with shit on your face.

'Sucking it up' and learning from others with much more experience is the right way to go forward. A good Zookeeper is never too proud to ask more experienced staff in the field; it is never a silly question. An animal carer cannot just do things and take risks because animals could die from this ignorance. Zookeepers may have a favourite species or feel more comfortable with certain animals, but the same care and respect needs to be offered to all animals. It's wise to respect people that make time to train Zookeepers and to take constructive criticism and advice. Neither of us ever had a problem with asking or answering questions from others. Not all Zookeepers have the same attitude, which is a shame.

As Zookeepers we never stop learning when working with animals, so there is no need to feel insecure. Although now we are very experienced Zookeepers, we both accepted this from the start and learnt not to be over-sensitive. From our training and experience, we know that Zookeepers will not be taken seriously until they usually have 3 years plus (full-time) working as a Zookeeper. Only then can you start to question items with experienced Seniors. It's not a good career move to do otherwise. We enjoy seeing other Zookeepers who are totally involved in their career inside and outside of the zoo, even on holiday visiting other countries.

Zookeepers continue to behave horribly, with another terrible and low act; leaving animal enclosures open to get someone in trouble or lose their job. When I started out in this world, my Senior Zookeeper had informed me of this and said she had experienced it herself. I was shocked that people would be so mean to each other, and ultimately put the animals at risk.

Letting animals out is dangerous to everyone, including the animals. These people have seriously lost the plot if they deliberately do this. I received this behaviour later on in my career and was more than shocked by this very desperate act. A difficult Zookeeper deliberately went out of her way to unsecure animals then reported it to a Senior Zookeeper to get me in trouble. It's certainly not a nice or normal place of work at times, but this also makes your workplace interesting! Your day is never the same, and it's certainly a learning curve that maybe we could live without.

Yes, some Zookeepers play dirty! Something we have both noticed over the years is that some Zookeepers are happy to take other Zookeeper's credit for their work. *'Monkeys see, Monkeys do'*. It's not pleasant when someone takes the credit after you have had a great idea or a solution, been proactive and got it done. Then, when on a day off, on leave or not in a meeting, it's been recognised by someone else. This is something I find very hard to accept. To avoid this, a Zookeeper should never take credit from another Zookeeper but just work hard and put their name on everything they produce. This includes daily reports, animal reports, health observations, diet sheets, routines, procedures, policies. Yes, sounds ridiculous, but you must in this environment. Over the years, we have seen and been the victim of other staff taking credit and playing dirty. Zookeepers have been two-faced and back-stabbed us for the limited positions in the zoo. A so-called friend has done this. It's hard to believe, but it happens and, yes, it's sad to report it in this book. However, I am being honest as it's a path that is not known as well as in other industries.

The dirty business of drugs is everywhere, including in zoos. A colleague friend who was working in a large zoo in Australia was really disturbed that some Zookeepers were arriving to work under the influence of drugs. She was annoyed they were doing this. These selfish, irresponsible Zookeepers were putting everyone at risk, and this is certainly not acceptable behaviour. It was a dangerous time for the animals, other Zookeepers and the public. Most Zookeepers are reliable and will not come in hungover from alcohol or drugs, or if not feeling 100% and working with dangerous animals, they will take the day off. Full concentration is needed at all times.

Unfortunately, I find it difficult to understand that someone would risk their job and everything else to a drug, but then I am not addicted to drugs. Like a lot of families around the world, we are troubled by this behaviour, and I have been directly affected by people that deal with drugs. My brother became a criminal plus a drug dealer and eventually became a drug addict and his life turned into a different pile of shit from the animal piles of shit I was used to! There is/should be zero tolerance for drugs in the animal world. My friend's story of the Zookeepers did finally get out in the media but only years later and random drug tests were brought into the zoo which hopefully would shake up these irresponsible Zookeepers.

I have worked in many industries and the zoo world is certainly a unique one. It is a challenging workplace with unusual characters and some difficult Zookeepers. There are clicky groups and some bullying is present from females and males. The environment of Zookeeping is raw, certainly not like working in an office. Animal people are passionate, so emotions can be triggered. Zookeepers are not always great communicators, they curse, they get upset and show a lot of frustration. I have witnessed this often and have also been caught up in physical altercations. Sorry to say, but a Zookeeper needs to be tough and not run to the boss. They must deal with their problems directly with the person. I have seen feisty Zookeepers,

I have experienced grabs, slaps and punches working in this environment, which is not always politically correct. I am an assertive person which can be difficult at times, but it's not aggression, it's passion and should be treated as an asset for improving the life of animals.

One day here in Australia, early on in my career, I experienced two male Zookeepers having a disagreement whilst chopping up fruit. It got heated, so I stepped in and advised the two experienced Senior Zookeepers to take time out and leave the area. This was sorted between them, with no bosses causing it to become a big issue. Another time, I heard about two female Zookeepers disagreeing on something. It got heated again, and one Zookeeper was grabbed and held up against the wall. This time, one of the Zookeepers ran to the boss, and it became a massive issue for them.

Then whilst I was working in the UK, a Christmas party for Zookeepers went wrong when a uni student turned up. This student's behaviour was questionable—drunk and flirty with a Head Zookeeper. His partner, another Senior Zookeeper, punched her out on the dance floor. This Senior Zookeeper was highly regarded, but she'd had enough. The uni student caused a lot of trouble creating this ruckus and then put in a victim complaint against the Senior Zookeeper! I took all these events in my stride, because they each had their reasons to express themselves and sometimes it's not always in a controlled manner. Sometimes it really is a 'dog eat dog' situation!

Unfortunately, I was caught up in a difficult situation with another Zookeeper that found it hard to follow instructions from more experienced Zookeepers. It was very obvious to us that not employing qualified, trained and experienced Zookeepers can cause unnecessary problems in this field. I have worked in 10 or more zoos and in my experience, with any 'Zookeeper performance' concerns, it is usually recognised promptly and taken seriously. This Zookeeper tried to intimidate me with a bullying attitude that was out of order. When the Zookeeper trapped me in a room and verbally took it out on me, I couldn't get away, but I would not take this ridiculous behaviour anymore. So I slapped the Zookeeper's face to stop that shit! This Zookeeper was like a Snapping Turtle (*just would not let go*). Be accountable for your poor work! Deal with it and learn from more experienced staff! It put all new experienced Zookeepers and Senior Zookeepers' reputations at risk, whilst we raised the zoo's animal welfare. Zookeepers performing at a low standard of work should be addressed immediately to avoid this challenge. The punishment I received for defending myself against this other Zookeeper was extremely high, but in my world, there is no time for this crap—only animal crap for Zookeepers!

All that said, I am OK in this kind of workplace—we all need to lighten up and not be so precious. I recently heard from one of my favourite comedians '*do not be so arrogant to think you deserve a life without people saying stuff to you that may offend you*'. The whole world needs to consider this for sure.

Zoo Management Behaving Badly

On my journey of working in different zoos in other countries, I learnt that there are certainly '*Rumbles in the Jungles*' in this environment, and they do not like media coverage. They will especially avoid any dirt on the industry. In order to keep bad stories out of the media, there appears to be an agreement with the local newspapers to only print upbeat stories about the zoo. Newspapers want to receive feel-good stories so they will avoid printing bad stories like escapes, injuries, deaths, animal theft, law claims and animal welfare issues, under the directions of the zoos. On top of that, it's made clear that us Zookeepers need to keep our mouths shut; we are informed that we cannot leak stories to the media.

So, when animals are stolen, the zoo would rather it was not leaked, and management makes it very clear to all working Zookeepers by calling a meeting to be reminded, even acting in a big brother bullying manner. When there are issues at zoos like bad animal welfare, we have found it risky to speak up to improve the conditions without serious backlash. Zookeepers are easy to replace with the overwhelming numbers that apply for each position advertised, but great Zookeepers with the skills, training, passion and drive–not so many.

I have done some research on this matter and managed to find a story that got out into the papers in the eastern states of Australia with a large popular zoo. Experienced Zookeepers, Vets and Vet Nurses were not being treated well. They were leaving and being replaced with less experienced, unqualified staff, causing animal welfare issues at this zoo. This zoo is a high-profile tourist attraction in Australia and receives funding from the Department of Tourism and Sport. Unfortunately, as Zookeepers, we are aware that any bad findings would certainly jeopardize a lot of money for the State with bad publicity. This situation was shut down as a high priority by management, but the animal staff and volunteers who had serious concerns were not supported. This was very disappointing. If experienced, qualified and skilled animal staff are leaving and the turnover is high, this should be taken seriously and looked into as the animals may not be receiving correct care. Often when this happens, it can be covered up as all departments want to shut the story down, resulting in the Zookeepers or the whistleblower jeopardizing their position. In this instance, it was investigated by Biosecurity Queensland and the Department of Agricultural and Fisheries, but apparently, and sadly, they found nothing withstanding. (*Of course they didn't, no surprise to us with this answer*).

It's important that everyone keeps their eyes open and reports any concerns—*go on, be brave for the animals. Keep your eyes open and report if necessary.*

Rhonda and Mike

When Mike and I got together, we found it interesting that even though I grew up in the UK and Mike grew up in WA, we both spent our spare time in a similar manner, like watching similar nature animal TV programs like *Tarzan, Skippy, Flipper, Elsa, Born Free, Dr Dolittle, Clarence the Crossed-Eyed Lion, Grizzly Adams* and *Into the Wild Jack Hanna* shows.

My true-blue Australian partner Mike, *(also becoming an endangered species!)* always wanted to be a Zookeeper. Mike was given heaps of freedom and spent most of his time outside amongst nature or at home caring for all his pets.

Eventually, our paths would cross over to share a future. Corny I know, but I was looking for my own tree house, in my own jungle with a Tarzan and Jane relationship and found something the Aussie style instead!

After 10 years working overseas, I returned to WA to my original zoo. On my first day back, I drove to the zoo in the madness of cars for 45 minutes from the north, arriving a few minutes before 7.00 am for the section meeting. I recognised a few people from before, but a lot of new Zookeepers were present. Mike arrived a few minutes later, travelling 45 minutes through rush hour traffic from the south. Both of us cursed about the traffic, the bad driving whilst everyone sat at their computers all in their own little sanctuary.

It was obvious to everyone right from the start that Mike and I were similar characters. We were like an Alligator and Crocodile, and the magnetic force between us was there as friends first, then as a couple later.

We both worked together on the Australian Section. Mike ran the Nocturnal House as the Senior Zookeeper, I worked as the float Zookeeper using all my different skills. We became good friends, having a similar work ethic, values, principles and passion for animals. We have both worked with many couples working in the same field together and have found it to be no problem at all. We both have worked hard and spoken up to improve items in this difficult world. We made people laugh, yes, we did with our big personalities, and once we spent more time together, we realised we had a lot more in common.

One was not supporting live export trade for many years. We both support farmers, but definitely not live export. Our Head Keeper couldn't say no when a few of us Zookeepers wanted to go out during our lunch break to support a demonstration at Fremantle harbour. We rushed around, took our uniform off, participated and then returned back to work. We thought it was important to be there. Other Zookeepers wanted to go, but like all events, people drop off when it comes to it, but we made a big effort to support it and enjoyed this experience. Mike feels strongly about this and has supported Animals Australia with banning live export for years.

Embracing a nice day out on Rottnest Island with the quokkas which have earned a global reputation as the happiest animal in the world by their smiling appearance.

Our relationship developed from good friends into a quirky couple. We kept it quiet for a while, but when we entered the zoo for a fundraising event one evening, selling animal art for the Silvery Gibbon Project it definitely started some chattering amongst the zoo workforce. The event was a good evening, we had fun supporting a good cause. Mike may have gotten a bit carried away and bought a few too many paintings. One of the Zookeepers that did a lot of the organising of the event, who received an injury on her arm whilst training the sunbears was present again. All Zookeepers like to support each other with special animal events like this. Attending the Gibbon Fundraising Event together 'let the cat out of the bag'. Everyone could see we were a couple. Now I was working on a different section in the zoo, but we met up for lunch. We were a force, two strong Zookeepers with big mouths dating and willing to stand up and speak out when necessary!

As a couple we do not get away much, but we have had some great short holidays and it's always in nature. Owning your own hobby farm means it's hard to get away. Living in Australia means there are loads of outdoor experiences to embrace. We have swum with Whale Sharks, which was incredible. We have snorkelled in a breeding turtle conservation area in the Ningaloo area. We have participated on eco trips swimming with dolphins. These trips are amazing; it's very good for the soul to meet other passionate people working in these areas that pass on their knowledge and enthusiasm for your trip. A trip to Cocos Island a few years ago for a short while was just lovely. We snorkelled off the island and experienced the wildlife in a very uncommercialised place. This island was also once a quarantine island for zoo animals coming into Australia. We saw all the old enclosures on one side of the island. These are our kind of trips out with the beautiful environment amongst it all.

We have also done Zookeeper field trips through the zoo or in our own time, for example, we have participated in numbat and woylie trapping/tracking. These opportunities do come up, and they can be interesting and fun to do.

 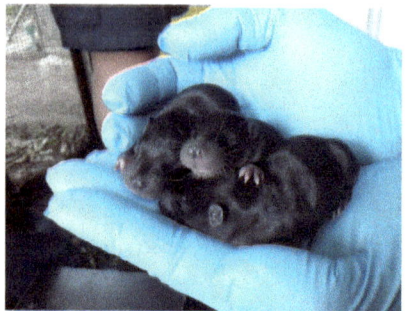

Mike participated in a field trip with other staff to collect ghost bats, resulting in bringing some back for the nocturnal house for a breeding opportunity with new genes. He also had the opportunity to trap the native water rat and bring some back for the zoo for a breed and release program. At one stage, Mike hand raised some native water rats for education at the zoo.

Whilst we were out on a trip in Karijini national park, we went night spotting with reptile Zookeepers. This involves them getting very excited when they spot a snake. Yes, an enormous venomous snake, taking photos, catching them up to have a good look at it. For me, spotting the cute mammals was more pleasing, but it was great to share all their excitement and knowledge in this field. The world of working with animals can put pressure on relationships outside the workplace. Loved ones will have to understand, as with many careers, being dedicated is not without a cost. The zookeeping roster means outside weekend events cannot be attended, including regular sports, events, going out late, public holidays and long weekends are not an option for the Zookeeper.

We both have worked on many Christmas Days, Boxing Days which are OK for us, but not so OK for partners and children. This can put extra pressure on relationships so special care is needed to prevent future problems. Many people's relationships in this industry have shown cracks, eventually causing break ups and heartaches. Like police and nurses, heaps of Zookeepers date and work together. There are limited places to work, so it's not uncommon to work at the same zoo together.

But finally sharing this life with someone special that enjoys the same interest as you is what everyone hopes to find, and when you do in this 'concrete jungle' life starts to feel right and has some meaning. Both being Zookeepers certainly helps—both understanding our priorities, choices and having the same values makes it easier. However, being passionate about this can also cause some heated moments between us. As Zookeepers with a combined 40 years' experience working with a huge variety of species in Australia and overseas has given us the opportunity to let people know the inside story. The ups and downs of choosing to work with animals in a unique environment presents massive challenges, but mainly due to the humans in it. Since we have been together, we have had chats about how choosing to work with animals has plenty of pros and cons. We look at other people around the world who are not into animals, do not own or work with animals. They go to work and come home and do not have pets. How easy life would be! No hardship and probably financially better off. But then we say, how empty life would be and how ugly the planet would be without animals. How weird and hideous would life be without the company of animals? It certainly would not be for us. Mike's mum loved animals and was deteriorating with dementia, but when animals were present, she certainly improved and it added life to her face.

Even when my mum died overseas in the height of COVID, my dogs could see I was sad and offered me some animal therapy and licked my tears.

It became a dream for us to run our own animal business, and after a few years of working together in a large zoo we decided to look for something else. We wondered how we could transfer our skills away from a zoo. First, we bought an established, egg hatching education program which involved delivering fertile incubated eggs to schools and aged care facilities to watch and learn from the chicks' hatching experience. This business kept us busy and certainly was popular, but after a few years we decided to sell it on and possibly set up our own animal therapy business. We could see that similar experiences could be delivered offering animal therapy to humans. After a few years, we had the idea of setting up a quality mobile animal close encounter experience which offered animal therapy to everyone, like prisoners, child protection, schools, aged care and childcare. We decided to sell our egg hatching business for a new future business we wanted to set up to offer animal therapy.

Then an opportunity came up to buy a small zoo just outside of Perth. This does not happen often, but we were keen and needed to investigate. When it came up for sale, we put an offer in after a few visits to see what the place was about. We were excited as we knew we could run our own zoo and had the correct background and knowledge, but the zoo needed heaps of improvement. Enclosures needed a lot of repair and standards needed to be raised for us to put our reputation on the line. But there was potential for sure. Our offer was not accepted. A higher offer from someone willing to risk everything bought the little zoo, and we hoped that the new owner did the right thing and improved the conditions for the animals that live there. It certainly needed work.

So we seriously considered our idea of starting up our new animal therapy business now. We knew with our years of experience working with animals there was a need for a good animal therapy experience for humans through mobile close encounter animal interaction, so we took the plunge in 2019 and set up 'Meet the Animals'. However, the timing was shit. We had heaps of bookings with aged care, childcare, schools, libraries, but COVID hit the world, and all this had to be put on hold.

We managed to keep afloat, diverting our audience to home bookings, birthdays in particular, wearing masks. These bookings kept us going until COVID was under control. Meet the Animals offers an experience of getting up close to reptiles, birds and mammals with professional, safe interactions. We take out around 15 species of animals, from pythons (snakes), bobtail lizards, frogs, a tarantula spider, dog, black cockatoo, chicks, guinea pigs, rabbits, rats, mice, ferrets, axolotls, stick insects and Dexter our popular Barn Owl.

Dexter is a barn owl. Through our contacts, we managed to acquire Dexter as a chick to hand raise under the guidance of our friends who run a bird of prey rehabilitation centre (WA Conservation of Raptors) and have specialised in this for many years. We had to gain the relevant permission and licence to hold this owl for education purposes. It was a joy to hand raise him, a real pleasure. We love this owl and gave him the name from the USA series *Dexter*. Hand-raising him with chopped up mice and chicks was very messy and bloody—a bit of a 'blood spatter' just like Dexter's job in this series we were watching at the time. Dexter comes out with us, and on the glove he gets up close to people. He is very popular with everyone. They cannot resist his heart-shaped face, clean white and cream plumage and calm wisdom. We have a variety of tame farm animals that we can take out for bigger experiences.

Here in the lovely Southwest of WA we have a retired vet who has worked hard to gain a relationship with the local farmers and abattoirs and rescues babies that are needed. Here they are treated and rehomed to hobby farms. We have taken on calves, raised lambs who have joined our other rescue goats, alpacas, pigs, horse, and donkey out in our paddock.

Being ex-Zookeepers, we can deliver a safe, professional animal close encounter. Whilst we are out with Meet the Animals, we can also offer good pet care advice and what pets are suitable for their family and their lifestyles. We also cover guidance on what to do if you find any injured wildlife in your area. Owning and running our own animal business means we have no boss (who is ignorant to this field like some of the management we've had) causing us unnecessary stress. We offer the best animal welfare to our animals. Our passion, good animal skills, and hard work is seen by all our clients and is recognised by rewarding us with return bookings every year. Running your own business is certainly not a pushover, You have to do everything, plus it's your reputation so you must always be on top form when delivering your service, but the good point is, all your hard work is for yourselves and not for bosses that really do not appreciate how you put your whole heart and soul in it when working with animals. Our Perth business was running well, heaps of bookings, and returned customers.

Then an opportunity came up for Mike; to take on a new project at a little zoo. They were looking for (*and certainly needed one*) an experienced, qualified Senior Zookeeper and it was in the rural area we were looking at relocating, away from the city. Mike decided the little zoo had potential for sure, but unfortunately not foreseeing that this zoo would cause us so much stress and exasperation. It was run under the local authority, and dealing with their attitude was the challenge we wish we had avoided.

Meet the Animals was put on hold whilst we both worked at this small zoo and relocated to the country life.

For Us All to Believe in Zoos

For us all to believe in zoos, and to continue to visit, feeling confident that they are a great place to drop in and support, we need to know everything, the mucky dirt as well. As dedicated Zookeepers we believe that good zoos are out there being run by experienced, qualified staff at all levels. We would like to empower everyone to monitor and make sure that zoos keep to a high standard and if not, what can be done about it. Knowledge is power, and in the zoo environment, it's not always easy to know the system they operate under, so the next few pages will give everyone the chance to know the guidelines to help monitor and support their local zoo.

It's time to consider important issues about zoos and all animal industries. We can do this by talking about the bullshit of the Animal World, not just the cute and fluffy side that is given out while the rest are kept quiet. For everyone to support zoos, we need to know everything.

To start with, there are private zoos, government zoos and even the odd local authority-run zoo. Some good, and some not so good. With social media now, everyone can catch and post images for the public's attention, spreading both a positive and negative portrayal of the zoo. Are the animals and Zookeepers protected whilst working in the Zoo World? That's our question, and we found the answer to this *the bloody hard way*.

It appears that, legally, animal welfare does not rank very high as a priority when it comes to going to court. Wow, that's a surprise for us. We can all scream and shout and try to improve it, but to the government, areas like conservation, farming, wildlife and animal attractions, zoos, wildlife parks or aquariums all appear to be rated very low on their agenda. They offer lip service and ticking boxes to look like it is. As experienced. Zookeepers that give everything to their job and will try to protect their animals, it does not appear to be the same for the Zookeeper from management. Zookeepers and those who work with animals are subject to multiple legal responsibilities depending on where they live. Here in WA, there is the Animal Welfare Act 2002 and the Biodiversity and Conservation Act 2016.

Everything looks good on paper. All zoos and wildlife parks can apply to join a number of organisations in their country, but it's not compulsory. When you enter a zoo, you will see if they are covered under one of these organisations. Here in Australia, it's the Zoo Aquarium Association (ZAA), who can be contacted with any issues first. All zoos come under Animal Welfare Acts, but the ZAA have other standards which must be adhered to. ZAA is an accreditation in Australia through which zoos and wildlife parks can apply for approval at an upfront and yearly cost. This will include an inspection, and the biggest value is that zoos can gain surplus animals from other accredited zoos more easily. In WA, there are about four zoos/wildlife parks that have joined ZAA while the rest have chosen not to.

Before we were familiar with this organisation, we thought highly of them. We believed there was something out there to support Zookeepers when needed. We hoped that they were not another organisation that didn't hold power for the animals and Zookeepers.

Other countries have the equivalent, like AZA for the USA, BIAZA for the UK, EAZA in Europe, and WAZA globally. If the zoo has joined one of these organisations, it means it offers or *should offer* a higher standard of animal welfare. However, once the zoo has joined one of these organisations, not all zoos under that organisation are ranked the same. There are 400 members in the WAZA and each year they hold a WAZA conference, an annual workshop for this industry.

This membership promotes cooperation between leading zoos, aquariums, national and regional associations as well as with leading wildlife experts, academies and universities. These conferences are very valuable, and you will make good contacts by networking whilst attending. WAZA provides support for species conservation management and husbandry of animals in human care, while encouraging the highest standards in member institutions. One could perhaps compare it to the United Nations but for animals!

However, from our experience, it seems that only when issues are highlighted by social media do this organisation increase their checks. An organisation like this should ultimately be able to regulate the standards before any untrained eye (the public) notices something that they need to report.

Unfortunately, we both had to contact this organisation, but hopefully, with both our experience, it was noted.

Placing Zookeepers into position without the correct qualification, skills, knowledge and experience is—or should be—unheard of in a well-respected, structured zoo with high standards, and more control should be considered in this area of employment. Zoos are a dangerous working place and practicing SOP Standard Operating Procedures is very important. We found working in this environment frustrating, stressful, dealing with non-animal management's attitude in thinking it was acceptable that anyone off the street can be a Zookeeper with no serious training or experience.

We are aware that every 3 years, zoos under this organisation have an inspection, but from our experience, the inspection is not in-depth, and any zoo can apply to come under this umbrella. We have seen and heard that when animal facilities receive concerns from the general public, it is acted on slowly and sometimes covered up, which is concerning.

Zoos or animal organisations that are not under the ZAA receive no inspection, so the standards are being relied upon by the Zookeepers and owners of the animal facilities. There is no monitoring of the experience, skills and knowledge of the staff. There should be random zoo and animal facility inspections by independent inspectors experienced in working in this industry for 20 years plus who really know what to look for.

In 2004, it was good to see that a story leaked out to the media. A popular local authority-run zoo in New Zealand showed serious animal welfare issues. Staff were also mistreated, with no support and the management ignored the Zookeeper's animal welfare concerns. This was raised with ZAA. Due to 20 current and past Zookeepers complaining to ZAA and the Ministry of Primary Industries, some action was taken. The zoo had received complaints six years earlier. Consequently, many Zookeepers left and were replaced with new Zookeepers, and now history is repeating itself. With the media once again onto it, they had to step in and sort it out. Like this one, many animal facilities cover up issues and avoid any media, so we know there are more, but all kept confidential.

In this case, they will now make inspections every three months and hold anonymous surveys. Let's hope that this shakes everyone up in the industry to take Zookeepers' concerns on immediately to prevent any animals suffering or dying from the delay. As Zookeepers, raising concerns can cause some incompetent managers to refer to you as troublemakers, ringleaders, foot soldiers or bad apples in the cart. It's ridiculous and not an excuse to ignore these issues. After all, we are dealing with living beings.

Around the world, local authority zoos have had issues; it confirms to us that the structure and lack of understanding of the demanding animal world makes it hard to run a zoo this way. Both of us have experienced working in zoos with poor conditions for the animals or Zookeepers.

Zookeepers can be put under immense pressure when they are working in facilities with limited funds, skilled staff, food or good vet care facilities. This is very stressful to achieve what you want and what you expect to deliver.

As experienced Zookeepers, we recommend to all the public, if a zoo here in Australia is not under ZAA then your first port of call with any concerns is The Royal Society for the Prevention of Cruelty Against Animals (RSPCA) as they have other standards which must be adhered to. However, the RSPCA are so overloaded with general domestic inspections that this is not the ideal solution. Besides, zoos are a completely different industry than domestic pet or farm care, so their inspection skills may be limited in this field.

Then here in WA, you have The Department of Primary Industries and Regional Development (DPIRD) who is the next port of call to contact. Then you have the Department of Biodiversity, Conservation and Attractions (DBCA). They mainly deal with native animals. All this might be boring as bat shit, but we all need to know so we can report any concerns to keep the standards high.

Each state and country will have the equivalent monitoring body. In the UK it is DEFRA. A lot of native animals here in WA come with licences that are issued through the DBCA. It's not easy getting animals into WA or Australia from overseas, even for zoos due to strict quarantine policies. The whole system can be frustrating. Wildlife Officers from DBCA who visit zoos and wildlife parks may have limited experience or knowledge of the captive animal husbandry in zoos. Their skills are more in the area of the legal aspects, compliance, policies, licensing requirements and the management of the land. We have worked with many DBCA staff, including Wildlife Officers, but recently we viewed a job advertisement for a Wildlife Officer for DBCA and the main requirements were experience in law and enforcement; nothing much about experience or knowledge or even passion for animals, so that says it all for us as Zookeepers.

Visitors from overseas will see that zoos in Australia are limited in the variety of species due to Australia's strict import and export laws and quarantine policies. These have not changed over the years and remain the same since the 50 and 60s. The variety of animals on display in Australian zoos is certainly different from overseas. This is a shame, as Australians miss out on seeing a large range of species. Unfortunately, due to the Zoo Regional Collection Plan, many animals are not encouraged to be kept, so once they disappear (die off), they are not replaced. Once these species of animals have gone from Australia, it will be very hard to get them back. It's certainly not easy to start up a zoo in Australia. Environment Australia, based in Canberra, holds strict import and export policies for Australia. These policies need to be reviewed as they are old and have not moved with the times. It seems like there are 'rules for the sake of rules', because they are so outdated. However, it is not a priority for the government to act on this. It's great that Australia has fewer diseases than the rest of the world thanks to the quarantine restrictions, but there's definitely room for some flexibility here. The general public, Australian citizens, are affected by this, and a change for different import and export policies would be greatly appreciated.

Maybe it's time for a change and for Environment Australia rules and policies to be updated. A good example would be for pet birds that are adored by their owners and would do anything for them. However, they are not allowed to be taken out or brought into Australia. This is a disturbing discovery for bird owners. I have been personally affected by these rules and have helped other people out by looking after loved pet birds whilst they live overseas due to the outdated export and import laws. Apart from Australia and New Zealand, no other country acts in this manner. Maybe it's time for an overhaul of the policies.

There are quarantine procedures that could be set up for these pet birds, just like any other animal, to prevent any disease. The world cannot prevent any disease coming into their country from wild birds flying over. Allowing pet birds to be quarantined to enter a country is common around the world, and it works, but here in Australia it is not considered.

We personally would like to reassure that Zookeepers around the world are making a difference every day. Perhaps it's not obvious to the general public or to some management, but it's there all the time and the animals will certainly know and appreciate it. Mike and I know that we have made many improvements over the years for all animals in captivity whilst working in this field.

One of my proudest achievements was whilst working at a rundown zoo in the UK that had been previously shutdown due to the zoo having animal welfare concerns. Within a few days of working at the zoo, I heard about a beautiful scarlet macaw parrot which had been put in a room on his own in a small cage the previous year.

He had become aggressive and no-one wanted to deal with him or had the time or skills to work with this bird. I spoke with the new Curator and offered to get him into the gift shop in a larger cage and do some training and interaction, as I knew he would come good and would be an asset to the zoo. I delivered this and then searched for sponsorship to build a big aviary to house him in for interaction with the public for the wellbeing of the animal and a great exhibit for the visitors. This bird was popular, and watching him enjoy his better life made a difference. At the same time, I also rescued another blue and gold macaw that was tame, and had an amazing life (in fact the house was converted to allow the bird to live and play through the house), but the owner was dying from cancer and just wanted his bird to be housed well on his dying wish. These birds were popular and watching them enjoy their new life as a Zookeeper making a difference gave me great accomplishment and pleasure.

For Mike, he has made improvements and a big difference to many animals over the years, staying at one zoo for 17 years. Mike always had an innovative attitude. After he did his own research and held meetings with his Seniors, he managed to implement a lighting change over to red lights from ultraviolet lights (black lights) that had been used for the nocturnal house animals for many years. This change of lights was an animal welfare improvement for the animals' eyes. The big benefit came when the animals displayed much more with these lights. Even though we do not work in those zoos anymore, knowing that we made a difference for the animals, other Zookeepers, the public, owners and management who all continue to benefit from our hard work is very pleasing.

Now that we are out of the zoo world, we can speak up and inform others without any restrictions. (Well, not really, but we can give you some ideas). We hope the story of our journey can help the reader understand what a Zookeeper does, and hopefully gain more respect. Not just anyone can fulfill this role— training and experience are needed to deliver good animal welfare. In all the industries we have worked in, the animal world is a challenging one, particularly the zoo world. It can be very testing and demanding (that's the humans). Managements of zoos certainly show disregard to this position at times by creating an environment that turns Zookeepers against other Zookeepers like gladiators fighting lions in a Roman arena!

Watching films, documentaries on TV about whistleblowers speaking out against companies, CEOs, management, government, even presidents or Prime Ministers interest us. We praise this, and more people should join together and participate in this action. Bad management and leaders in the world can seriously damage people's and animals' lives. The constant covering up is real bullshit.

This attitude can be a big problem when working in zoos. Incompetent management in zoos can damage Zookeepers and animals' lives. The majority of Zookeepers are way too scared to expose this bad behaviour and toxic environment we have to work in. The backlash if we raise any concerns is harsh. Zookeepers will not risk their already competitive jobs, and the threat of this keeps animal staff quiet... unless you are Rhonda and Mike! We have put our head on the 'chopping block' because we are confident. We knew our job well, were great at it and addressed the requirements, but in the end, we were totally disrespected along with the animals' needs.

History tells us that if we do not speak out and ignore these problems, nothing will improve or change. Making people more accountable (though this is not easy) is the only answer. It's our duty as animal lovers to shout it out so everyone can see and make their own judgment about what is right and what is wrong for the animals. We have noticed that in the human race there will always be people that put their own needs first over principles and not practice what is right and stop what is wrong. We find these people hard to respect and work with. Speaking out as Zookeepers has certainly helped. Some zoos are evolving for the better, and good signs are now showing in 2025, but it's an ongoing process.

Mike and I feel strongly about speaking up. We're sick of the serious wrongs which will continue if we sit back and let it happen, especially when dealing with animals, children and aged care. Neither of us can turn a blind eye; we stand up and raise concerns and make recommendations. But speaking out is always at a cost, and we have both suffered stress and loss for doing so, including our position as Zookeepers. We can both say as great Zookeepers we delivered our jobs 100% and more. We can be true to ourselves knowing we offer the best animal welfare through our great husbandry skills, and we will always be fully committed to this and even if we are not in the industry anymore, we are watching these places. We have both witnessed zoos that have held a title of a great zoo for many years to falling into the poor zoo category after a few years due to not having the correct management or staff running it. Not controlling the collection plan well has led to many empty enclosures. Outside events, like wars, world pandemics and animal disease (TB, bird flu) has also caused complications. We were totally shocked to see this can happen. Just maintaining a zoo without the skills and knowledge will finally show the world and cause public concern to support zoos. This is why its so important for the correct people with the knowledge need to continue.

The last zoo we both worked in has certainly left a bad taste in our mouths which we are trying to wash away, but it will be a while before we can. Putting our animal therapy business on hold whilst taking on a new adventure of working in a little run-down zoo sounded like a good idea at the time, but now, looking back, what were we thinking? It could have been a great career move. Mike was thinking he would work there as the Senior Zookeeper until retirement, but working under the 'Utopia government system' certainly was unrealistic for running a zoo. We hadn't really experienced this way of thinking, but it was present, and it nearly destroyed us.

Utopia *is an ideal place or state, usually one that is unrealistic or unattainable, a place of ideal perfection, especially in laws, government, and social conditions, an impractical scheme.*

We have found this behaviour in zoos, wildlife parks and land management departments under the government. We both enjoyed the Australian ABC *Utopia* comedy TV series that shows this attitude is common where nothing gets achieved and they waste a lot of good money.

When we arrived at this little zoo, it was obvious that all the staff working there were 'self-taught', and the zoo lacked serious, trained staff and lacked care. Direction, motivation, dedication and passion were not shown. We knew what was required and cracked on to get 'the show on the road'. We went above and beyond for this little zoo working long days, pulling in all our skills, knowledge, experience and training into this place to raise the animal welfare and improve the whole business. We have often wondered why we worked so hard for the local authority. Ultimately, it was because no one else was. We cared and loved our position as Zookeepers. We both can stand tall, (well, if that is allowed!) knowing that in every job we have held working with animals, we have put our whole heart and soul into it for the love of the animals. We improved the zoo by gaining more animals, offering better animal welfare, better exhibits and an improved visitor experience and the great feedback was appreciated. We felt proud to be part of the new, improved local zoo. The animals looked happier and behaved appropriately. We raised the standards of the diets, health, exhibits, shelters and handling skills. We made a massive difference, especially for the animals. Unfortunately, the whole experience of working at this zoo under poor management with no idea and lack of interest caused us a lot of stress and left us feeling deflated.

Working in these conditions was bloody impossible unless you just become lazy and drift through your job, being OK with doing the minimum amount. After bringing the zoo up to scratch, we had a very important ZAA inspection booked for the zoo. Most people would agree that this laid all our reputations on the line. On this particular day, Mike and I were running around 'mad as a hatter' as we had a few days of preparation to improve this park for the inspection. We managed to teach the new inexperienced Zookeepers, all the volunteers and everyone to be keen as a beaver. The team joined together, 'working like dogs'. They came in on a public holiday the day before to fine tune the place. Mike and I rustled up some lunch and refreshments and everyone was proud of what we had achieved. When I say everyone, that does not include any management (all non-animal background). They just did not get how important it was and just looked on.

Like any kind of inspection, it's horrible and stressful. On this big day we were ready and boy, Mike and I were so glad we had all the experience we did to address some of the questions. We knew and were confident in our field—if you were not, the bullshit would show. The inspection had come because the zoo had joined ZAA a few years prior and no inspection had been done before. The downside was that the inspectors had not seen how bad the place was when we started and what we had done. The test showed us that non-animal management really did not have any clue what was required for a zoo, and it confirmed that we really did know our stuff in this world. The inspection was a success, and that was exciting for us Zookeepers and volunteers.

This zoo proved to be no sanctuary for us. What we both know for sure is that zoos are no place for people without the love for animals and understanding of the concept of a zoo. Everyone knows that this should be *dead as a dodo* in zoos.

With our experience, we are very much aware that managing a zoo requires balancing the provision of excellent animal management and care with an optimal visitor experience and quality customer service. We have found that it's important for all levels of management to be 'animal people'. Working in an animal attraction, zoo or wildlife park, you would expect people to be passionate about animals and have experience and training. My comment may sound obvious, but both of us know from experience it's a constant challenge to work with these non-animal people, wasting heaps of energy that could be used on the animals.

Not all zoos are the same, but what we have found is that privately owned animal facilities can be very good; in fact, some are excellent. Some of these places are our valuable contacts. They are excellent because they are totally committed, and this is their world. These owners have worked their way up from the ground, holding the passion, drive and experience to make a good animal attraction. It gives up hope after feeling very cynical about zoos from the last working place we had to be involved in.

Larger zoos that have employed trained and experienced animal staff and have a good structure also work. Many zoos are top heavy and would benefit with less office management and more on the ground (*yes, that's Zookeepers—the important staff*) so they can offer a better animal welfare service.

Some zoos have been created or run without the correct people behind them. They have a poor understanding or no background with animals and can lack the respect, values, passion, drive, skills and knowledge. This generally applies to positions like the CEO, some management, human resources, administration, cashiers, education/outreach departments and/or marketing and media departments. In worse case scenarios, there are some Zookeepers that fall into this category as well.

Thankfully, the majority of people working with animals have chosen this path and have been trained by experienced professionals in this field. It's a lifestyle, owning or working with animals. We value and know the importance of it all and enjoy the company of animals (and not so much the human!).

Having said that, non-animal people can have an important role working in the zoo. Using their skills in Guest Services Agent positions, Public Relations positions and Special Events positions can be helpful and beneficial as long as they work with the Zookeepers. They need a good insight of the animal and the public requirements to run a successful zoo.

This is where the battle lies, and this is one reason which encouraged me to write this book: the pure frustration of working in this unique world with some management that lacks the understanding or respect for Zookeepers needs to be told so hopefully this can be avoided in future zoos.

"The difference between humans and animals... animals would never allow the dumbest ones to lead the pack." Winston Churchill

"The species that survive are not the strongest species nor are they the most intelligent, but rather the ones who best adapt to change." Charles Darwin

This saying goes both ways, for the animals and the Zookeepers.

Since going through a hellish, stressful time working under the local authority in a zoo, we imagine how amazing it would be to work in a zoo owned by Zookeepers. Owners that have the knowledge, and passion. How refreshing and fulfilling would it be for any Zookeeper and for the animals?

I am aware that there are zoos out there with this in place, so there is some hope. I had the opportunity to work at a well-regarded zoo in the

Channel Islands. This zoo was set up in the 1960 by Gerald Durrell, who was a British naturalist, writer and Zookeeper. He wrote books to fund his zoo. When I gained a position at this popular zoo, many years after he passed away, the structure of the zoo and reputation were still there and good to see. This zoo had a different feel to it. Gerald's vision was still present; it was definitely more about conservation in particular islands around the world with a high diversity. It was exciting working at this zoo. The opportunities to participate in field work were high in some exotic places like Mauritius, Madagascar, South America. I enjoyed talking with other Zookeepers who had been out there working directly with many species, like the cute, charismatic, and oddly human-like lemurs in the field with the native people. It sounded amazing, and I held so much hope listening to them all. The other important issue that this zoo performs is encouraging native animals back into the zoo grounds. For visitors it is a lovely place to walk around heaps of nature surrounding you because of the volunteers and Zookeepers working together to create this haven. By simply adding a lot of plants, building habitats, it showed the difference. It was impressive to bring back native mammals, birds and reptiles to add to the zoo experience.

Another famous zoo, this time here in Australia, is the zoo that was set up by the Irwin family. The famous charismatic Zookeeper Steve Irwin ran the zoo and became a legend. Unfortunately, after his death, this zoo has been in the media with questionable staffing issues. Many experienced and qualified staff left due to this situation. The story was shut down after a so-called investigation was done.

In Western Australia, there are a couple of animal attractions run by Zookeepers, and they certainly display their animals at a higher standard and we both respect these organisations. Miami Zoo in the USA has a Zookeeper that worked his way up for 40 years in the industry and is now the Communication Director of the zoo. When you see this long-term Zookeeper out in the zoo or on TV etc., his enthusiasm is catching and just a dream to watch. This gem of a Zookeeper does TV shows representing the zoo. He knows his stuff and shows the world how important his mission is. This Zookeeper turned Director does not just talk the talk but walks the walk. He is very inspiring and what an honour it would be to work at this zoo with such a brilliant mentor. I wish there was more of this; we can only hope.

Yes, there is a life after being a Zookeeper, but you will miss all the animals and your unique position in this role. Zookeeper skills are transferable. There are some interesting jobs out there, though not always known.

Mike took on a Cameleer position with a good company. The boss was skillful, and Mike gained more specialised knowledge in the camel field.

We both worked as dog handlers for 3 months, working closely with two truffle dogs each, looking for truffles out in nature all day with just the company of the trained truffle dogs,' just bliss' but unfortunately, the 200km round trip each day was not sustainable every year to participate in. We made some good friends and learnt some new skills. In fact, we now foster the same truffle dog from the farm every year for 8 months. This very loving rescue working dog joins our pack, whilst resting from being a hardworking truffle search dog in a growing gourmet industry.

Someone once said to us that 'you two do not do well in captivity!' That certainly does sum us up. The concrete jungle, massive human population and political correctness is taking over the world like an 'invasive toxic plant' that keeps on strangling the life out of us.

We know after years in the animal field that, like some humans, not all animals do well in captivity, so this is always considered when housing different species in zoos, wildlife parks and sanctuaries. All Zookeepers need to ask themselves, 'how are the animals doing?' and when you know better you can do better.

That's why training and experience are necessary to deliver amazing husbandry at a very high standard of welfare to the animals you are working with. I am grateful to have worked with Mike over the years in a big zoo, a small zoo and in our own two animal businesses. I have really seen and respected Mike's devotion to his Senior Zookeeper position. At all times, whatever the weather or situation, he has offered the highest standard of Zookeeping; nothing is too much when it comes to animals.

After working in 10 or more zoos around the world as a Zookeeper, I can certainly say this with full confidence, and I am proud to witness Mike's amazing husbandry. Lucky animals!

Saving Animals After Being a Zookeeper

There is plenty we can do to be involved in improving all animals that live with us on this planet and you do not have to be a Zookeeper to achieve this and one of our favourite projects is right here in WA.

There are all sorts of people with different lifestyles and knowledge, working hard to save the unique Black Cockatoos that live on our doorstep. You certainly do not need to be a Zookeeper, vet, or wildlife carer to get involved. These birds need everyone to get on board to save them from falling from this big blue sky. How could we let them disappear from our landscape? It's very disappointing to watch them decline. We have both got involved with this mission, either through the zoo as Zookeepers or in our own time as volunteers. Once you have got up close with these gentle giants, you will not be able to resist their charm. We have both been fortunate to have done so, including having our two tame black cockatoos here with us on our farm.

We suggest to anyone that is interested in helping these majestic birds to just get out there and volunteer. There are three main organisations to help the black cockatoos. The first is Kaarakin which is based in the hills in Perth. This is a registered charity centre for the Black Cockatoos and is purely dedicated to rescuing, rehabilitating and releasing Western Australian injured black cockatoos. They educate the public on the plight of WA endangered black cockatoos. The aim is to increase areas of natural habitat for WA's black cockatoos, protect existing habitat and rehabilitate degraded disused land. They are always looking for good volunteers, and it's a great place to gain skills and offer your time to a great cause.

Carnabys Crusaders is based in the north of Perth, a registered charity for the Black Cockatoos dedicated to support the recovery, breeding and preservation of habitat that supports WA native Black Cockatoo species. Their goal is to ensure the survival and promote awareness around the required preservation of natural habitat to support our native Black Cockatoos.

The owner, Dean, specializes in providing artificial breeding tubes to local farmers, landowners, even zoos. (We called him in for a talk and set up two tubes in an enclosure in the zoo, which led to breeding a chick for the first time here). These added nesting tubes in the wild will boost the numbers of these amazing birds. It's not a long-term solution to the viability of the species, but it certainly helps. It's very important to provide more natural feeding and breeding habitats for the black cockatoos, so working with the government is an ongoing activity.

Native Animal Rescue in the northern suburbs of Perth has a Black Cockatoo Flight Path Facility that was opened due to receiving a good grant from Lotterywest. This facility allows NAR to receive Black

Cockatoos and put them into isolated care and eventually progress them into an open flight area where they can regain their wing strength, ready for release back into the wild. Flight Path provides accommodation for up to 9 Black Cockatoos in isolation, and a further 30 + birds in an open flight area measuring 300 square metres.

We support them where we can with donations either financially or in other ways with our time, education, and signing petitions. You will see from some photos in our book that there are some amazing artists and photographers in WA. Who have captured the essence of these amazing birds and help with auctions of their work and were happy for me to display in my book. The other way we are going to help the wild Black Cockatoos is to gain some artificial breeding tubes on our property, which we hope to organise soon. We have trees and a state forest backing onto us, so we experience these birds on a daily basis.

We also look forward to donating a percentage of every sale of our book to Carnaby Crusaders, a valuable conservation cause, which is highly important to us both.

by Irene Young

by Sally Edmonds

Photographs by Martine Perret

Now Let's Go to Court

*F*or us, *'life keeps on punching'*. Yes, in our final years of being Zookeepers we are now having to fight with lawyers by taking the local authority to court. Yes, it's tough on both of us but it's necessary as two qualified, experienced, skilled, passionate and very dedicated Zookeepers to stop this history of pushing it aside and not valuing animals and skilled Zookeepers. It's going to cost us plenty of money, time, hard work and stress, but as Zookeepers it's always about the animals.

We have both gained a good variety of experience working in the animal environment industry to express this opinion. We have found that some average wildlife parks, zoos, petting zoos, and animal attractions lack the skilled people to run, maintain them, and do not offer the best care for the animals in the correct manner. They do not know the requirements, and these places should be monitored and held accountable at all times. Why? Because the zoos that are performing the high standards are being dragged down by the low standards of these zoos. Hence, the skeptical general public and animal lovers will continue to dislike zoos if the standards of all zoos are not kept high.

Our last experience in this field has made us feel that all the bullshit we had to take, the stress from the lack of knowledge and disrespect for our Zookeeper occupation, needs to be raised. All the bullying that large organisations deliver to put the fear factor into staff/Zookeepers to shut them up is just not acceptable.

Yes, we are prepared to go to court if this is not settled. It's not easy; we are up against local authority management, and we have been made aware that most of them have changed their positions since we have left; the classic act. But the managements are sticking together to save each other's arses spending the local communities' rates to fund it. All this could have been avoided if they let us do the job we are trained to do. We have been going back and forth between their lawyers and our lawyers. It's very draining and affects our mental health. It has taken over our life and delayed our new life.

I must admit that I find it very painful and overwhelming at times, and have had my meltdowns in private. We really just want it all to stop, but my inner self will not stop as we need to speak up for the animals and make sure animal caretakers practice better standards. Unfortunately, animal welfare issues do not appear to come under a specific law for us Zookeepers in this case. This really sucks. Do we need to be a whistleblower to get our point across?

Now, the definition of a whistleblower, is an individual who, without authorisation, reveals private or classified information about an organisation usually related to wrongdoing or misconduct. It generally states that such actions are motivated by a commitment to the public interest.

So WTF! We need to make people aware of this; it's not good enough. But we know that organisations like the RSPCA have been fighting this for years to have better animal welfare for all animals. The law stinks, and heaps of issues do not fall under standard laws when taking someone or some organisation to court. If the public knew how much it's taken from us and to see the huge effort and loss this has caused us over the years. They would understand that we need to fight animal organisations that show a lack of skills/knowledge, which holds back zoos, creating a lack of confidence, which certainly can help justify why some people have a negative view on zoos.

The whole process has been extremely disturbing for us. The financial cost will be high as management appears to play dirty games and will try to discredit us to cover up their lack of knowledge they hold in this area. Any decoy will be used. It's not easy practicing mindfulness, dealing with lawyers and this crap most days, but it has to be done. Certainly, having this court case over our heads means it's difficult to move on. Our successful animal therapy business is still on hold and we wish we had the mental strength to start it up again, but this time in the South West. But it looks like we will start to take bookings and deliver our close encounter animal experience after the court case in the new financial year.

A lot of people support, admire us and think we are brave to fight this wrongdoing, or is it stupidity? Most people in other industries, non-animal industries say, just get another job and work for people that appreciate your efforts, but that's not possible. There are no jobs like this around. It has affected us massively, so that is why we are speaking up. We love visiting a good zoo and we will continue to watch for any bad practice in zoos. We will make sure all zoos lift their standards so that zoos can be respected around the world and enjoyed by everyone. But mainly the most important reason is that all the 'ambassador animals' kept in captivity are offered the best life they can under a Zookeeper's care.

Right up to getting this book finished and published, we found out that our legal claim was settled out of court 1 month before the trial. We thought this would happen; it's common, apparently. It's sad that our zoo career had to end like this, but it's exciting to know we can now move on and put our valuable skills, personalities to good use, like writing this book, running our own business and being involved with fellow people that have the same values, lifestyle as we have chosen. Sharing the same common goals in life, which is to share this planet with animals and do the right thing by them all, this will sometimes make us enemies and upset some people, but it's all about the animals, that's it, nothing else.

Life After Being a Zookeeper

The best decision for our wellbeing in our 50s was to downsize from our two properties to one and relocate out of the city to the country. Now we sit on our verandah off our tiny home, overlooking our 72 acres located in a lovely part of Western Australia, thinking "This is the good life".

We are becoming more self-sufficient, growing our own veggies, and learning new skills, like being apiarists (being a beekeeper with our two bee hives) and enjoying our free range chooks and freshly laid eggs. We live off the grid; we have tanks to collect rainwater and have our solar power that produces our electricity, so no electricity bills for us.

Our dam is the focal point where we enjoy playing with our dogs, and the rest of the animals often join us. With the company of five high energy dogs (three are rescue dogs) and approximately 150 pet animals and a demanding parrot sitting on my shoulder, Mike and I appreciate what we have over a cuppa and say country life is definitely for us. Not having to mix with the growing 'wokness, political correctness' population unless we choose to. Being able to surround ourselves with resilient, like-minded tribes. Enjoying nature and practicing mindfulness when we can. Living in the magnificent southwest of Western Australia, with the beautiful beaches, ideal climate, wineries, local produce, lush farmland and mighty forests, plus the more relaxed lifestyle, certainly makes it more palatable and achievable.

Now that we have more time to enjoy the rural life, we are thinking about improving our riding skills. Mike and I have done some horse riding, but would love to be more confident and possibly gain two suitable stable horses to blast across our land. How amazing would this be? Maybe this will be our next adventure, we keep on thinking maybe we are too old, but then I say nope, even though Mike has ridden more camels and elephants as a Zookeeper than horses, we both definitely want to be trained by experienced horseman or horsewomen, as we know training from the correct people is the only way it should be.

"I found the key to happiness. Surround yourself with animals and stay away from idiots."

"Dogs do not judge, they do not gossip, they do not lie, dogs are true friends." Dr. Mary B. Fossum

Having your own space to breathe, by looking out over our land with a beer and taking in the peace and quiet, is our kind of medicine. There is a big blue sky, dry landscape, but the perfect winter temperature of 23 degrees accompanied with wild animals; kangaroos, emus, noisy cockatoos, even eagles, plus the annoying Aussie fly sharing the land with all our pets. Now we are 'living the dream'. What different scenery I viewed 35 years ago in the UK, with green fields, a lot of rain, and a British summer high temperature of 23 degrees. I was surrounded by different animals—hedgehogs, deer, badgers, squirrels and little perching birds, plus the odd wasp to spoil the day.

All countries have their own unique animals and landscapes and their own successes and disaster conservation stories. For us, wherever we live, it will be in our blood to help animals when needed.

With reflection, we close our book, asking 'what makes a person want to be a great Zookeeper? We believe it's having a massive passion for animals, the drive and need to have a positive impact on animal welfare, encouraging natural behaviour by providing enrichment and being part of the conservation taking place at zoos. We know that working with animals is ultimately the highest privilege, and it's a Zookeeper's need to see the animals under their care every day developing a connection with another living being rather than a human. Whoever owns a dog, cat, horse or parrot or even a mouse will understand and cherish that special connection by having them in our lives. It's funny to say, but after some thought, maybe zoo animals are all special 'emotional support animals' for us Zookeepers. With a mutual respect that should be treasured, holding a real pride, whilst performing our day-to-day duties in a unique field as a great Zookeeper.

Even though we have put forward our honest story, down to the dirty business of being Zookeeper, (dirt certainly comes in different forms) it's an amazing story to tell and a wonderful world to be part of and we hope that zoos continue to grow and that all sorts of people in the world will continue to enjoy and benefit from 'a good day out at the zoo'.

For us, this great final quote that we found is from one of our favourite British comedians who does heaps of animal charity work and makes massive donations to animal charities and is right out there exposing animal welfare matters.

*"**Animals don't have a voice. But I do. A loud one. I'm a f***ing big mouth. My voice is for them. And I'll never shut up while they suffer.**" Ricky Gervais*

This quote really made us laugh. Yes, we both have big mouths, too. Some people in this world could say how vulgar, but his direct talking hits you hard and really does get the attention that needs to be gained. Well done, Ricky.

Whilst going through our journey of the good and bad, it inspired me to write this book to give a behind the scenes of our lives as Zookeepers and to also reassure the public that the majority of Zookeepers are proud and love their position. They will deliver everything they can for the animals under their care. They will always put the animals first, whatever, just like we both have over the 40 years in this industry and always will.

The journey will continue for us, and our life together with all the animals is good. We are grateful that we are strong and united in this and continue to stick up for the animals and all good Zookeepers to the end. Keeping quiet is not an option for us; 'to fight the good fight' it has to be.

This old saying means to do your best and do what is morally right. Mike and I believe in this, especially when you are working with animals.

Enjoying some time on our land with our animals.

We continue sharing our wonderful animals through animal interactive experiences to help increase the love and respect for all animals around us.

Here we go again, offering our animal interactive experience to all ages, this time in the lovely South West.

A New Generation of Zookeepers

We will continue to inspire as many people, especially children to cherish animals and if they want to be a Zookeeper, like Mike's great nephew who admires Mike and just enjoys animals so much and may, one day, also want to choose this lifestyle.

Some kids do better out of the classroom amongst nature, this feeds their curiosity which leads to compassion to all animals, sparking inspiration to learn more about the environment. We leave all the incredible animals in their hands to protect and preserve where they can.

A NEW GENERATION OF ZOOKEEPERS

Here are our little helpers that show great potential to love and appreciate all animals great and small.

So You Want to Be a Zookeeper?

Most Zookeepers around the world intend to specialise down the track of their career once they have been fully trained up and been exposed to a variety of species. But I knew gaining as much experience as possible at the beginning of my career was necessary and made me more employable. It's more than important to be flexible to work on all sections of the zoo. Each section is very different, some are more hands on than other sections.

When we both started out, we certainly knew that for entry level Zookeepers we needed to know the structure within a zoo and quickly learnt the important steps to becoming a respected Zookeeper, the below information can be interesting for anyone to know what it takes to work in a good zoo.

- **A Zookeeper position** – You will be in training for the first 3 years of an apprenticeship. You will need to gain a Zookeeper Certificate III or Animal Care Certificate or equivalent. As a Zookeeper you have to gain training and experience with these qualifications.

- **A Zookeeper position** – with 3 to 5 years' experience should have skills that can deliver good husbandry and offer good animal welfare at any zoo.

- **A Senior Zookeeper position** – 5 years' experience and up will have supervision duties and will train other Zookeepers. You will have responsibilities like running a section, holding a studbook, and being responsible for all animal welfare.

- **A Head Keeper or supervisor position** – 10 years' experience and up will have more supervision and managing work in the field with all the Zookeepers. Overseas the care and management of all animals within the section.

- **A Curator position** – 15 years up, you will be dealing with a collection of animals, exhibits, Zookeepers, policies, procedures, licensing, animal transfers and budgets. This also involves being mindful of zoo goals, and how the education programs and exhibits reflect these goals. Usually you will have a Curator for each section in a large zoo.

- **The Vet Department** on site will have a few experienced, qualified Vets at different levels and experienced, qualified Vet nurses to support them.

- **Section Directors** – large zoos will usually have a Director for each section; Vet Director, Mammal Director, Director of Operations, etc.

Here you would expect these positions to be held by Zookeepers that have progressed to these positions and have full understanding of the operations of a zoo and high standards of animal welfare.

- **Zoo Director** – Their job is to oversee the operations of the zoo as a whole. They are the face of the zoo to the public. Their primary job will consist of raising funds to continue the zoo's operation. Most directors will have little to do with animal care. Many come from a business background.

- Some large zoos now offer a course in a Zoo, Certificate III in Wildlife and Exhibited Animal Care which is the pathway to a career as a trainee Zookeeper. This course offers class sessions and practical assessment, and the cost is approximately $8,000.

Our Do's and Don'ts for Aspiring Zookeepers

All Zookeepers will/should receive formal training for many years through mentors. People entering the world with a Zoology degree or Vet Nursing qualification is a bonus and certainly offers some background and help, but it does not make you a Zookeeper.

1. Please gain some experience working with animals—paid or unpaid experience is one of the most important prerequisites to becoming a Zookeeper.

2. Gain work experience at vets, wildlife parks, RSPCA, animal welfare organisations, dog training, wildlife rescue centres, kennels, animal breeders, stables, animal groomers and farms, etc.

3. Get some experience within the zoo environment. Join to be a volunteer or gain some work experience at a zoo organisation.

4. Volunteer at a Wildlife Rehabilitation Centre. Do the weekend course and get registered as a wildlife carer to gain some great skills.

5. Be prepared to work without pay in the animal field (a volunteer). This is an expectation that shows commitment. This will result in learning heaps, making contacts and having skills to offer and will make it more likely to gain a paid position in the future.

6. Treat all volunteers with respect, you have been one and a good volunteer is a great asset to a Zookeeper and to the animals.

7. Gain a Certificate II or Certificate III in Animal Care and/or a Certificate III in Wildlife and Exhibited Animal Care. A Vet Nursing qualification or Conservation or some Biology degree are other ways of getting appropriate qualifications for Zookeeping. A Zookeeping Certificate was only available through a zoo when we started. Now anyone can gain this qualification online by a course without working in a zoo. You can get work experience in zoos if you are studying a relevant course.

8. While a degree in conservation, zoological, animal care, environment, etc. is great, this is a practical job, so having experience working with animals or a background in farming can be more beneficial than a degree.

9. Accept that being a Zookeeper is not a self-taught job. It is learnt on the job by training for years, and it's important to be aware of this and learn as much as possible from a variety of people that

have been in the animal industry for years.

10. A large part of a Zookeeper's responsibilities is presenting information to visitors, so some training or building up confidence in this area is very useful. Zookeepers need to be able to work outside in all weathers and be OK with it. It's not an office-based job.

11. In this industry, the first 1 to 3 years are spent as a Trainee Zookeeper. Only then does a Zookeeper have something to offer when applying for a position in zoos. A saying is 'get some time up before you speak up'.

12. Accept that you will always be learning in the animal fields. Making many contacts in the field with different knowledge is important. If you are not sure, ask, never protect your ego and jeopardize an animal's welfare because you do not want to ask and learn from others in the field.

13. You will need to learn to be comfortable with a variety of animals, big and small, and will gain confidence as you receive good training over the years to work with many species.

14. Most zoos and wildlife parks have sections. Everyone is on the Zookeeper team but separated into Zookeepers within a section. These include the Bird Section, Farm Section, Carnivore Section, Ungulate Section, Elephant Section, Primate Section, Mammal Section, Exotic and Native Section, Nocturnal Section, etc. A

Zookeeper is always learning, and it's good practice to move around the zoo, gaining as much experience and knowledge as possible. Do not try to specialise too soon.

15. Going on field trips, trapping, tracking and any conservation field work is fun. Plus, you learn heaps and gain contacts. Overseas conservation work is everywhere. Grab it with both hands—it's rewarding and exciting.

16. Learn to use a rake, a hose, a screwdriver and basic equipment. These will be used on a daily basis. A Zookeeper should not expect other people to perform these maintenance duties.

17. Most zoos will advertise yearly for their employment pool for casual Zookeepers. Applying and getting ranked to be called upon to be trained and used as casual Zookeepers is the way to get in the door.

18. Once a contract is secured, there are plenty of other Zookeepers in direct competition, so it's a stressful place to keep a contract or get another one. It can create a backstabbing environment, and some people can behave badly with other Zookeepers. If a permanent position becomes available, Zookeepers both outside the organisation and those in present contracts apply for this one position. Often the casual Zookeepers that are doing well do not sell themselves enough in the interview, or naturally do not know how to play the game or fight dirty. Unfortunately, good people can miss out due to this unpleasant situation.

19. When you are finally a Zookeeper, please do not become a lazy Zookeeper. Don't just do the rounds. Do extra jobs and think outside the box. As with all industries, there are Zookeepers who take the job for granted and do the minimum. These people should leave and let a person that has the enthusiasm to enjoy this career go above and beyond and appreciate their position.

20. Some jobs are advertised on Australian Society of Zookeeping (ASZK). Most Zookeeping positions are looking for 2–3 years or more experience for basic Zookeeping positions. We advise head down, bum up and 'get some time up'.

21. Zookeepers or people working with animals will often face births, sickness, injuries and death of their animals, so learning to deal with emotions is necessary. It's very upsetting, but it's a fact of life in this field.

22. Zookeepers have to work weekends, on a roster, gaining public holidays off, school holidays off etc. and can be very difficult.

23. Zookeepers working overseas will face other responsibilities on top of normal duties. In a colder climate, the weather causes more work to provide animals with the correct conditions. These zoos have many heaters and lamps. In a country that has warmer climates, a cooling system is provided, such as ice blocks or water sprinkler systems, to keep the animals cool. Some animals may need to be moved off display in different seasons.

24. Pay around the world varies as a Zookeeper, but what we have noticed is that the pay is low for what you do, or expected to do and the skills you hold, wherever you practice. Here in Australia the pay is much better than the pay you receive in the UK. I certainly experienced that.

For all non-Zookeepers, knowing and understanding what our day consists of might help to persuade the skeptical visitors to the zoo. Knowing on your next visit that most Zookeepers work hard to meet all the requirements of their animals, and our main goal is to display the animals to a high standard. Our advice to all visitors who come into our world that feel there is room for improvement, then please speak up to the zoo and then to other organisations for answers.

We have personally noticed that impressive zoos will employ experienced, skilled, qualified and knowledgeable Zookeepers, and this shows through the whole zoo when allowing visitors to embrace the unique experience of a zoo.

Zookeepers Make the News

dustries," says Judi Anderson, senior account director of the Waite Career Centre in Melbourne. It is also worth reading *Job Prospects* by Rodney Stinson, and referring to the government website, www.dewrsb.gov.au, a leading indicator of job opportunities and a source of general employment information.

Test the Waters

"Get experience first to confirm that you are going to be suited to a certain industry or profession," says career consultant and author Michael Creagan. Here's how:

• *Volunteer.* If you're thinking about nursing, volunteer at a hospital. Radio broadcasting? Read for the blind.

After leaving school, Rhonda Barbut became a secretary. But when she and her partner migrated from England to Perth nine years ago, she developed a deep love of Australian native animals, and started working as a voluntary wildlife carer for CALM (Conservation and Land Management).

"I often took kangaroos and possums to the office," says Barbut. "Fortunately my boss was very tolerant." Soon, she enrolled at TAFE to study environmental practice. Even before she had completed the year-long course, she was offered employment at Perth Zoo. Now 34, Barbut has been a full-time zookeeper for over two years, and still spends most of her days off as a volunteer at two wildlife sanctuaries.

Creature feature

The bond between human and beast is a vital part of Perth Zoo's success with endangered and exotic animals.

IF A work colleague decided to pee in front of you in the middle of the office, chances are you would not be impressed. But Michael Cranley could not have been happier than when Tricia, a girl he had been working with for six months, finally relieved herself in his presence.

It's probably worth pointing out that Tricia is a 47-year-old Asian elephant and the star attraction at Perth Zoo.

Unlike most workplaces, social urinating is encouraged in the zoo's elephant enclosure. Cranley remembers Tricia's first public pee with the nostalgic fondness of a parent recounting his child's first steps.

"That was a bit of a thrill for me; that's when she finally accepted me," he says with a proud smile. "A lot of people think she is scared when she is roaring and urinating, but that's actually elephant greeting, so when she finally does that it's like being accepted into the group."

So much for shaking hands. This touching, if slightly unhygienic, story is just one example of the rich tapestry of relationships between animals and people that make Perth Zoo one of Australia's best. These bonds enable zoo staff to develop a broader understanding of the many endangered species that call the zoo home.

One of the strongest relationships exists between the elephants and their keepers, the only staff within the zoo dedicated to just one animal.

"A lot of the other keepers in the zoo do actually work with other animals fairly closely, but they never develop a bond like us," explains Cranley, a senior elephant keeper who has been working with Perth Zoo's pachyderms for six years.

Standing beside a Jurassic Park-style gate outside the elephant enclosure, Cranley tries to talk professionally about his work as two trunks snake playfully through the bars trying to reach the slices of bread he has stuffed in his pocket.

"It takes a long time for the mutual trust to work," he says. "You are looking at six months minimum before you feel half safe around an elephant. The first six months, you have got to be very careful that they don't squash you or push you up against the walls."

Elephant society revolves around complex codes of social behaviour and the sheer size of the zoo's biggest animals reinforces the importance that these social codes are followed.

"You have to have a mutual respect; you have got to realise what these animals are capable of," Cranley says. "You have got to give them love and affection, but you don't do too much pampering. If you get into the idea that these are big pussycats, you are going to get hurt."

The big pussycats certainly must be handled with a degree of caution.

Kitoko, the zoo's resident cheetah, was hand-reared by staff at South Africa's De Wildt Cheetah and Wildlife Centre and this close keeper contact was continued when she moved to Perth in 1999.

"The main reason we have maintained that relationship is to be able to do medical procedures and treatments with her without having to sedate her or give her an anaesthetic," exotic mammals keeper Kathy Starr explains.

"The advantage of that is huge because with most of these animals, obviously, you need to anaesthetise them to handle them. We can do vaccinations, we can check her ears, we can check her mouth. Even the things we have done that have been unpleasant, she knows that they are probably of benefit to her."

Kitoko would be high on any child's pet wish list and the relationship she has with keepers like Starr closely resembles an owner-pet relationship to the untrained eye.

The keepers play with her to stimulate wild play instincts and encourage good behaviour through stroking, petting and talking. When Starr demonstrates this, Kitoko responds with loving nuzzles of her head, an occasional lick and a purr that sounds like a V8 engine.

Michael Cranley has his hands full with Asian elephant Tricia.

But this relationship is carefully structured to ensure Kitoko is not totally domesticated. It also emphasises the keeper's dominant role to minimise the considerable danger the 42kg cat could pose to a person.

"She is definitely not like a dog or a big cat," Starr says. "In a lot of ways, she is still very much like a wild animal and has a lot of strength and a lot of power and we have to respect that."

This physical contact creates a much deeper keeper-animal relationship than that which exists with the other big cats.

"The lions... there's no hands-on scratching or anything like that so you don't really get to develop that relationship," Starr says, casually adding: "They see you probably more as a food source."

Not all animals are as endearing as an elephant or a cheetah, but strong relationships benefit even the most creepy creatures.

Senior reptile keeper Glen Gaikhorst relishes contact with cold-blooded, scaly reptiles, but the kind of relationship depends on the type of animal.

"The relationship with a crocodile — there's really not going to be a relationship because there's going to be some healthy respect given towards that guy," Gaikhorst stresses.

"But for animals that you handle more, you get to know their behaviours as individuals. You get to know intimate

details of them, or when they are about to slough [shed their skin] or when they are hungry. It's not like a cat, where it can just come up to you and know individual people."

With snakes, the type of relationship depends largely on the breed.

"Boa constrictors are pretty bland, I suppose, in their behaviour," Gaikhorst says. "They don't give away much. But diamond and tiger snakes, you really get to know individual snakes based on their behaviours."

The deepest relationships are formed with snakes that star in the zoo's Keeper Talks — hands-on demonstrations in which keepers and animals team up to educate members of the public. Visit captains: "It's keeper calls me and says that such and such an animal is not too itself today, that can actually be quite a significant observation."

Zoo conservation Simone Vitali, who worked in private practice before arriving at the zoo six years ago, sees amazing similarities between keepers and doctors: patients when dealing with patience.

"It can become quite a challenge, but also fun, to try to work our way around the challenges that these animals give us."

She says strong keeper-animal relationships are crucial to provide effective health care for the animals.

"It's important for [keepers] to be emotionally involved with animals in the sense that they are picking up changes in behaviour," Vitali explains. "It's a keeper calls me and says that such and such an animal is not too itself today, that can actually be quite a significant observation.

"The keepers' deep knowledge of their animals can also help provide enormous the difficulties posed by reluctant patients.

"It can become quite a challenge, but also fun, to try to work our

way around the challenges that these animals give us," Vitali says. "When you worm a dog, you give an owner a wormer and say, 'Make sure he gets it with a meal' or whatever. When we worm our rhinos, it has evolved into a great production.

"We had great difficulty in [polyethylene] and we had the longest conversation the difficulties and said, 'They really like mint, so maybe we could come up with a peppermint flavouring.'

"We perpetually flavoured their medication and tried that and eventually we had to give up and try a burst-in preparation. But that in itself requires that the keepers get a front-end loader into the enclosure and remove all the manure piles before we start so we don't get any chance of re-collection.

"So something that with dogs is just taking a medication, in rhinos has become a major song and dance, which I think we are finally on top of."

Mike as a Head Keeper

Coasts exhibit is big Aussie puller

Rhonda drawn 9,000 miles

By ALLAN TUDOR

THE REPUTATION of the £7million marine wildlife attraction at Torquay has spread world-wide — even before it opens on Monday.

The chance of working at the Living Coasts exhibit at the Beacon was too much of a chance to miss for Aussie zoo keeper Rhonda Barbut who has travelled half way around the world to do just that.

Rhonda made the 9,000-mile journey from Perth in Western Australia to be senior keeper looking after penguins at Paignton Zoo's new attraction.

She came to Britain last year to do work experience, spent two days at Paignton Zoo and fell in love with the place.

She said: "The chance was too good to pass up."

Rhonda, in her early 30s, worked at Perth Zoo for five years and volunteered as an animal carer in her spare time, rescuing, hand rearing and rehabilitating kangaroos, parrots and possums.

She appeared on an Australian wildlife TV programme which is due to be aired here in the autumn.

In addition to her duties at Living Coasts, Rhonda is keen to help out with the evening badger watch sessions at Paignton Zoo.

In 2002 she attended the Gerald Durrell summer school at Jersey Zoo and organised a keeper exchange at Bristol Zoo.

She then came to Paignton to work with the bird department.

Rhonda said: "This is a unique opportunity to work on a great visitor attraction. Zoos today have a big mission to educate the public on conservation and environmental issues. I find it very rewarding to be involved in this."

■ **WORLDWIDE ATTRACTION:** Aussie keeper Rhonda Barbut, left, with colleague Chris Inman.

Rhonda as a Senior Keeper

This was the zoo that was made into a film.

Acknowledgement

So much thanks to all the good people (great mentors) that shared their knowledge and passion with us both whilst working in this field. To all the great Zookeepers out there, making animals' lives in zoos the best they can. We thank anyone that supported or trained us and offered their skills, in particular my partner Mike, a great Zookeeper who worked his way up to Head Keeper over the 20 years working with a large variety of different animals to me! We jointly respect each other's skills. We agreed to share our real experiences as Zookeepers and write a book for future aspiring Zookeepers. Finally, and possibly mostly, we would like to acknowledge all the amazing animals we have had the privilege to be with.

I would like to thank all the non-animal people that suggested and supported us in getting our story down, to hopefully show what it's really like working with animals and in particular in the Zoo World.

From two passionate Zookeepers who believe good zoos continue to have a place for us all to visit and support.

www.ingramcontent.com/pod-product-compliance
Lightning Source LLC
Chambersburg PA
CBHW061726070526
44583CB00024B/3019